Developing Parenting Programmes

Celia Smith

The National Children's Bureau was established as a registered charity in 1963. Our purpose is to identify and promote the interests of all children and young people and to improve their status in a diverse society.

We work closely with professionals and policy makers to improve the lives of all children but especially young children under five, those affected by family instability, children with special needs or disabilities and those suffering the effects of poverty and deprivation.

We collect and disseminate information about children and promote good practice in children's services through research, policy and practice development, publications, seminars, training and an extensive library and information service.

The Bureau works in partnership with Children in Scotland and Children in Wales.

The **Joseph Rowntree Foundation** has supported this project as part of its programme of research and innovative development projects, which it hopes will be of value to policy makers and practitioners.

The views expressed in this book are those of the author and not necessarily those of the National Children's Bureau or the Joseph Rowntree Foundation.

ISBN 1 874579 88 1

Published by National Bureau Enterprises Ltd, 8 Wakley Street, London EC1V 7QE

Revised edition published 1997

National Bureau Enterprises is the trading company for the National Children's Bureau (Registered Charity number 258825).

Typeset by Books Unlimited (Nttm)

Printed and bound in the United Kingdom by Redwood Books, Wiltshire BA14 8RN

Contents

List of tables

List of figures

The author

Celia Smith is a freelance researcher, formerly a Research Officer at the National Children's Bureau. She has worked in the field of child and parenting care in both the statutory and voluntary sectors, since 1974. She is author or co-author of several books and reports including *Day Nurseries at a Crossroads: Meeting the challenge of child care in the nineties* (National Children's Bureau, 1994) and *Confident Parents, Confident Children: Policy and practice in parent education and support* (National Children's Bureau, 1994). She is co-author with Gillian Pugh of *Learning to be a Parent: A survey of group-based parenting programmes* (Family Policy Studies Centre, 1996).

Acknowledgements

During the course of the review which produced the material for this book, many organisations and individuals responded to requests for information. Some are those listed in Appendix I, but there are also many others who remain anonymous, but whose contributions were nonetheless valuable. I was able to meet with a number of experts and practitioners in the field of parent education, and I am most grateful to all who gave of their time so willingly. The 60 participants at the seminar held in March 1995 provided invaluable feedback at an important stage of the project, and were able to highlight and discuss the issues which seemed important to them.

Perhaps my greatest debt is to those programme leaders, and more especially the parents attending the courses, who allowed a researcher to sit in on sessions as a 'fly on the wall'. This experience added greatly to the understanding of the processes involved in these programmes. It also provided opportunities to talk directly with mothers and fathers about their experience of parenting programmes, and to discuss some of the issues involved in facilitating these group programmes with some leaders.

Work on this project was greatly enhanced by the involvement and expertise of Dr Gillian Pugh, and the support of Dr Ruth Sinclair. Three people commented on the earlier drafts of this book: Professor Sheila Wolfendale, University of East London; Hetty Einzig, Parenting Education and Support Forum; and Christine McGuire, National Children's Bureau. Their constructive comments were most helpful.

Finally, this study would not have been possible without the financial support of the Joseph Rowntree Foundation, who funded it as part of their Family and Parenthood programme.

Celia Smith
March 1996

Preface to revised edition

The groundswell of interest in parenting programmes shows no sign of abating. Indeed, there is a growing recognition that most parents welcome help with this most difficult job. Professionals from all sectors are increasingly seeing the need for locally coordinated and resourced policies on parenting. In several areas this important topic has been built into Children's Services Plans. Parenting is no longer being treated only as a personal and private issue, but also as a political one – there is a growing view that the upbringing of our children needs to be a concern of the entire community and not just of parents.

Some parenting education programmes have taken on board the pleas to maintain high standards of practice by measuring programme content against suggested values and principles, and ensuring that evaluation of programmes is taken forward. One research project at the National Children's Bureau is setting out to explore the different expectations which course organisers, facilitators and parents have of parenting programmes.

The Parenting Education and Support Forum is just completing its second year of operation, with a huge agenda to tackle with minimal budget and staffing. The Parenting Forum has become the focal point for the collection of information about parenting education and support, for its dissemination through conferences, seminars and newsletters, and for the encouragement of networking between professionals from a wide range of disciplines.

This new edition will hopefully continue to stimulate debate and discussion about the many issues involved in parenting education.

Celia Smith, July 1997

1. Setting the scene

'Bringing up children is perhaps the most challenging and important task that most of us perform. It is a lifelong commitment – sometimes described as the only job we have for life – and how well we do it is likely to have a continuing impact on future generations, playing a significant part in shaping the values and attitudes that young people take into their own adult relationships and their approach to being a parent.' (Pugh, De'Ath & Smith, 1994, p.9)

This book is about some of the ways in which parents can be supported and assisted in this important 'job for life'. The purpose of the book is to describe and analyse a particular form of parent support and education – group-based parenting programmes, courses and materials. Its intention is to provide information about what is happening in this field during the mid-1990s in the UK, commenting on the range of programmes available, their aims, content and methods, the people involved in promoting the programmes and leading groups, and their effectiveness. The book will be of interest to health, social services and education personnel who are involved in one way or another with parent support and education; to voluntary organisations whose work takes them into similar fields; and to parents themselves. For those who want to move into this area of work, we hope it will provide an overview of the programmes available, and stimulate ideas for planning and implementation.

The programmes which are the subject of this book are referred to throughout as **parenting programmes**. Alternative terms in common use are 'parenting skills programmes', 'parent education programmes' or 'parent training programmes'. Each of these was rejected for a number of reasons: 'parenting' is much more than just a set of skills, neither does the process involved in learning about parenting seem to be adequately described by the terms 'training' or 'education'.

1

What we are specifically describing here is a complex process of raising awareness about parenting by means of participating in a series of group sessions whose overt purpose is to allow parents to find ways of improving their parenting, or to feel affirmed in their own parenting methods.

Before describing the survey which provided the material for the book, this first chapter looks at the broader context of parenting itself. Parenting has been described as a practice 'as old as the origins of human life itself'. It is 'a process of interactions and relationships intended to nourish, protect and guide each new life through the course of its development' (Bavolek, 1990, p.1). As such, this process has a vital influence on the way in which children develop and become the citizens of tomorrow and, indeed, on the way in which they in turn parent their own children. Most people take on the challenging job of being a parent with very little preparation or training. Until relatively recently, parents have been regarded as being naturally equipped for this important task. On the other hand, over the years there has been no lack of advice to parents on how to bring up their children, much of it contradictory and dependent on the changing norms and fashions in society, as well as the influence of successive professionals and experts.

The task for the parents of the 1990s is possibly even harder than it has been for others before them: parents in the 1990s are likely to find themselves confronted by a number of issues which were unknown to them as children, such as the level of violence and the representation of sex as displayed on TV, the easier availability of drugs and alcohol, and the concern about the safety of children in the environment. The extended family is less likely to be on hand to provide help and support; today's parents are more likely to come from smaller families themselves and may not have had the practical experience of caring for younger siblings from which earlier generations learned; more parents are likely to be parenting alone, or in re-structured families, with the resulting pressures which that can bring. Society has huge expectations of parents, and yet at the same time undervalues the role of parenting; the pressures on parents to perform, to bring up perfect children and not to make mistakes, are heavy and may induce guilt and anxiety. No wonder, then, that some parents find it increasingly difficult to know what is expected of them and how they can match up to those expectations.

Structural factors, such as poverty, poor housing, unemployment, family conflict and changing family patterns may compound, or even precede, these difficulties. A number of other themes impacting on parenting have emerged recently: children's rights have become more prominent; the concept of parental responsibility has been enshrined in the Children Act 1989, and is also integral to the new Special Educational Needs Code of Practice; the role of fathers has been given more emphasis; the need to respect the varying child rearing patterns of different cultures has been recognised; criminologists are increasingly coming to see the value of preventative work based on family support and parenting education in reducing crime levels (see, for example, Utting and others, 1993 and more recent initiatives of Crime Concern); the increasing number of women combining work with family responsibilities has tended to put more pressure on families; the UN Convention on the Rights of the Child underlines the concept of parents' responsibility for their children, rather than absolute rights over them. It also gives power to children's decision-making in the family, including respect for children's views and for their evolving capacities. The impact of all these factors compelled the International Year of the Family in 1994 to highlight the need for support for families at different stages of the lifecycle and in a variety of different ways. Similarly, there have been a number of recent calls (for example, Audit Commission, 1994; Utting, 1995; Pugh and others, 1994) for more resources to be allocated to preventative rather than remedial family support services. There has also been renewed emphasis on the effectiveness of preventive family support work in reducing child abuse. Hearn (1995), for example, highlights the risk of polarising family support and child protection work by treating them as alternatives, rather than mutually supportive and complementary activities.

Parenting: the most difficult job in the world

Before going on to explore the ways in which parents can be helped and supported in their difficult task, it is important to consider just what constitutes parenting. Is it a set of skills which can be easily learned? Or is it based on relationships between family members? Do we really know what effect parents have on their children: and is it not a two-way process, with children having a feedback effect on parents? Most people would probably agree that all these questions should be answered in the affirmative: parenting is a complex function involving relationships, communication, social skills, practical skills and the acquisition of understanding.

Many professionals have described parenting in terms of the basic needs of children which parents try to meet. Cooper (1985), for example, summarises these needs as:

- **basic physical care**
- **affection**
- **security**
- **stimulation of innate potential**
- **guidance and control**
- **responsibility**
- **developing independence**

Bavolek (1990) sets out the 'building blocks of parenting', on which his nurturing programme for families is based:

- **bonding and attachment** – the process of establishing an unconditional positive regard and acceptance of the child;
- **empathy** – the ability to see the world through another's eyes, and to consider the other as an equal, described by Bavolek as the single quality most critical to the overall growth and well-being of the child;
- **self-awareness** – for to be empathic to the needs of others, one needs to be clear about one's own needs;
- **touch** – a gentle, calm, nurturing touch which communicates to the child a sense of trust, kindness and security;
- **discipline** – or setting clear limits for children;
- **unconditional love honesty and respect** – for 'parenting is the process of helping children feel accepted by people without regard to their behaviour';
- **developmental knowledge** – knowing what to expect of children at their various stages of growth and development.

How, then, can parents begin to find a way to meet these and, indeed, many other needs of children? How can they aspire to become 'good enough' parents in the face of such formidable lists of needs? The concept of the 'good enough' parent, a phrase first used by Donald Winnicott (1964), is now commonly used to describe the state to which most parents try to aspire. It is generally accepted that there can be no such thing as the perfect parent, we have to settle for second best in aiming to be 'good enough'. Furthermore, there can be no single set of rules by which all parents should abide in order to bring up the

Table 1:   'Good enough' parents

'Good enough' parents are building up their **knowledge** about:

- human health and development, and particularly child development and what to expect at which stage;
- where to go for help;
- their rights;
- common ailments, and how to cope with accidents;
- the education system.

They are developing certain **skills or attributes**. Many of these are social skills, developed over a lifetime, which all adults need if they are to function adequately:

- they are authoritative, rather than over-protective, permissive or authoritarian;
- they offer their children love and acceptance, and are sensitive to their needs;
- they have confidence in their children's worth and abilities;
- they have appropriate expectations of their children;
- they find time to share experiences with their children – having meals together, playing games, going on outings;
- they are consistent, reliable and dependable, providing a stable and secure environment where rules are clear;
- they can set appropriate boundaries, provide adequate supervision and encourage their children to set their own boundaries;
- they can communicate openly and honestly, listening and reflecting;
- they can make decisions and accept responsibility for them;
- they can cope with stress and deal with conflict;
- they can see things from their children's point of view;
- they avoid harsh punishment, but reinforce good behaviour.

They are also developing practical skills, in managing the home and the family's finances, and combining work with family life.

They are developing **understanding and self-awareness:**

- of themselves as parents and of their needs;
- of their values and attitudes and how these impact on others;
- of how their own upbringing affects their ability to be parents.

(Source: Pugh and others, 1994, p.56)

'perfect child'. Every child is different, every family is different in terms of cultural and social outlook, in parents' own upbringing, in their view of what sort of adult they would like their child to grow into. Given the need to recognise the differing goals and values of parents, the social and cultural context in which families exist and the individual characteristics of children, Pugh and others (1994) have set out a portrait of 'good enough' parents (see Table 1).

The concept is that of an ongoing 'journey' during which parents are acquiring along the way **knowledge, skills and attributes, and understanding and self-awareness** in order to move towards being **confident, competent** parents. This concept of developing self-confidence and self-esteem is, as will be seen later, an important feature of many group-based parenting programmes.

Parenting education and support

Although most parents manage well most of the time, there are periods and occasions in the lives of the majority of parents when extra help and support is welcome and, in some cases, essential, in order to assist the smooth functioning of the family. The review by Pugh and others (1994) describes a very wide range of approaches to family and parent support, some providing support in the home, others in the community and yet others in schools; some use a one-to-one approach, others an informal group method, others a more structured group technique. Many are multi-purpose and able to respond flexibly to parents' needs. The authors suggest an overall definition of parent education and support in Table 2.

It is not always useful, or easy, to categorise approaches to parent education and support, or to attempt to draw boundaries between them. But, we do so now since it is the rather more formalised, group approach to parenting education which is the subject of this book. Moreover, these parenting programmes which this book is about are different from the parentcraft classes, the antenatal groups, or the parents' drop-in at playgroups or family centres.

The parameters of this study were so constructed as to include only those programmes which are explicitly concerned with helping parents to improve parenting skills, which use a group work approach, are relatively structured and formalised, and which are replicable with other groups of parents. Clearly,

Table 2:   A definition of parent education and support

- A range of educational and supportive measures which help parents and prospective parents to understand their own social, emotional, psychological and physical needs and those of their children and enhances the relationship between them; and which creates a supportive network of services within local communities and help families to take advantage of them.
- It should be available to all parents and prospective parents, boys as well as girls, young men as well as young women, fathers as well as mothers.
- It is a lifelong process and as such will have a different emphasis at different stages of the life cycle.
- Its emphasis should be on individuals' roles and relationships in the here and now, as well as on their future roles and relationships.
- The overall aim of parent education is to help parents develop self-awareness and self-confidence and improve their capacity to support and nurture their children.

(Source: Pugh and others, 1995, p.225)

we had to omit a wide range of broader support work with parents, some of which may be directly or indirectly linked with the improvement of parenting skills or may lead to parents asking for, or agencies deciding to offer, something more specific in this area. It also omits the undoubted supportive effects for parents of meeting together to reflect, discuss issues of the moment, or even to undertake a quite different activity in a corporate, sharing manner. The close links and relationships between all these forms of parent support are shown in Figure 1. The programmes which are under the spotlight in this present study are represented by the central part of Figure 1. Around this, and interlinking with it, are a number of other organisations and agencies which have an interest in parent education, and use a range of different methods, including parents' groups, to provide it. Indeed, as later chapters will show, many of the agencies and professionals in the outer part of the diagram, (for example family centres and health visitors) make use of some of the published programmes which are the focus of this study and are represented in the central area.

Before moving on to these *educational* programmes, it is important to acknowledge the work of agencies which *support* parents in a variety of ways, since all are likely to have a direct or indirect effect on parents' self-confidence, knowledge and

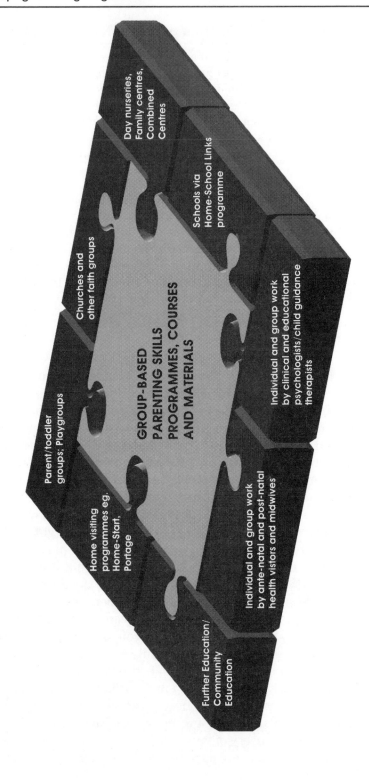

Figure 1:   Providers of parent education and support

understanding. In the area of advice and information-giving to parents, for example, telephone helplines, such as Parentline, have grown in number and provide opportunities for parents to discuss problems in confidence, and to be in charge of the conversation themselves. Home-based approaches, such as that provided by Home-Start schemes, and Portage, can provide support which is carefully tailored to each family's needs. Some forms of group-based support, like parent/toddler groups, are very informal and provide opportunities for mutual learning and peer support; other informal community groups, such as playgroups, toy libraries and groups run by churches and other faith communities, aim to reduce parents' isolation as well as providing play and learning opportunities for their children. Other, more formal types of group support sometimes grow from these beginnings. It is increasingly possible to find examples of multi-agency collaboration in the provision of support for parents. One example is in Peterborough where projects for parents and young children have been set up with resources from social services, education, the city council and the health authority. Another example is in Croydon, where several agencies (education, social services, probation, health, police, church and voluntary sector groups) which are all addressing different aspects of a common problem, have formed themselves into a Responsible Parenthood Committee. This has enabled different agencies to share knowledge, and sometimes resources, and to be subject to shared evaluation and monitoring.

The 600 or so family centres in the UK provide a wide range of support to parents and children. What Holman (1992) describes as the *client-focused model*, which works mainly with referred families and has a strong 'professional/client' ethos, is still the most common. Both Holman and Cannan (1992) suggest that the *neighbourhood model* and the *community development model*, offering a broad range of services and promoting user participation, are more effective in terms of promoting parents' self-confidence and self-growth. Staff at most family centres, and other parent support projects such as those operated by Family Service Units, would say that they are responsive to the needs of the particular parents using their resources, and that this sometimes means setting up the more formal parenting skills courses on which this book primarily focuses, as well as more informal approaches.

The whole area which has come to be known as home-school links is also important in the support of parents in a range of ways. This may perhaps focus initially on the role of parents as their children's first educators, and in the support of their children's learning, but frequently extends to the development of parents' groups focused on a range of topics according to parents' interests and wishes to extend their own learning. A specific focus on parenting skills sometimes develops from such schemes. Examples can be found within many local authorities, such as that currently in operation in a number of primary schools in Humberside, where parents have highlighted the need for help with behaviour difficulties in their children.

Aims of parent education

Parent education has been defined as 'a systematic and conceptually based programme, intended to impart information, awareness or skills to the participants on aspects of parenting' (Fine, 1980, p.5). The aims of parent education are said to be 'to effect change in parent role performance' (Brim, 1959, p.20), and by another author to 'upgrade child care practices of parents in the home' (Schlossman, 1976, p.438). As later sections of this book show, the goals, format, methods and materials used in parent education differ widely. Despite this diversity, there does appear to be some common purpose amongst the goals which the majority of programmes attempt to help parents achieve:

- to develop greater self-awareness;
- to use effective discipline methods;
- to improve parent-child communication;
- to make family life more enjoyable;
- to provide useful information on child development.

Professional advice and education for parents is rooted in a wide spectrum of theoretical approaches and research findings. Approaches overlap, complement each other, or may even be contradictory. They differ in their emphasis on particular aspects of the parent-child interaction and relationships, on the aspects of family life and difficulties on which they focus, those areas that they omit altogether, and the age of the child to which they apply. As will be shown later, these parenting programmes tend to be based on an amalgam of research findings, theoretical background and current societal views. Such diversity and complexity of method is probably important, given that the needs of different groups of parents also vary widely, and what is suitable for one set of parents may not be so for others. In order to bring some element of unity to such diversity of approach and method, it would seem helpful to ensure that parenting programmes are based more on principles than on prescription. A set of possible principles is illustrated in Table 3.

Table 3: Principles for group-based parenting programmes

- Diverse family patterns should be acknowledged and respected.
- Cultural diversity should be acknowledged and respected.
- Parents' existing skills, experience and knowledge should be built on, rather than starting from their failings.
- Programmes should be relevant to parents' own needs and planned in cooperation with parents.
- Programmes should be delivered in a style which is relevant and appropriate to the needs of parents.
- Programmes should be relevant to fathers as well as mothers.
- Programmes should be relevant to the stage of parenting in which parents find themselves.
- Programmes should recognise the effect children have on parents, as well as vice versa.
- The values and principles on which programmes are based should be clearly stated.
- The aims and objectives of programmes should be explicit and measurable.
- The results and outcomes of programmes should be constantly monitored and recorded and parents should participate in this process.

These principles are derived from a similar set of principles suggested by Pugh and others (1994, p.69) for parent education and more general support. They are also amplified by some of the findings of this study, which point to the need for further consideration of the quality of parenting programmes. This list is, however, offered at this stage as a basis for further discussion rather than as an authoritative set of principles. Such principles can, perhaps, be of use in assessing the quality of parent education programmes, and Chapter 7 explores this idea further.

However, even assuming that such a set of principles could

lead to a common overall approach, the *way* in which parent
education should be delivered, by whom, what skills and information are most appropriate, and at what point in time,
continue to be hotly debated. Such debate is illustrative of one
of the key dilemmas at the heart of education and support for
parents: is it a means of *social control*, encouraging conformity
and adherence to the status quo and reinforcing stereotypes?
Or is it a means to *social change*, empowering parents to
increase their self-confidence and gain control over their own
lives? Furthermore, it is, perhaps, pertinent to remember that
there is some evidence in the literature that parent education,
unless sensitively offered, can have some negative effects, such
as raising in parents feelings of guilt, anxiety and dependency.
Allan (1994), for example, argues that, although welcomed by
participants, an Australian STEP programme had the effect of
reinforcing certain dominant beliefs and stereotypes of motherhood and fatherhood. Another example of a negative outcome is
the Parent Education Package (Hewitt, 1991), a health visitor
intervention which, although popular with parents, produced
no behaviour change in their children, and some parents actually reported more anxiety about potential problems as a result
of the intervention.

Group-based parenting programmes

The development of parenting programmes for groups of parents in the UK owes much to earlier research and practice in
the USA, in particular two main programmes: Systematic
Training for Effective Parenting (STEP) developed by
Dinkmeyer and McKay (1976, 1982); and Parent Effectiveness
Training (PET) developed by Gordon (1975). More recently
Bavolek and colleagues during the 1980s developed a model
which emphasises the nurturing role of parents in developing
relationships with their children. Pugh and others (1994) found
that there had been a considerable expansion in parenting education over the last ten years, both in the form of published
materials and in the involvement of various organisations, professionals, church and other faith groups, and community
groups in the delivery of parenting courses to groups. It would
appear that there is a growing awareness of the strengths of a
group-based approach:

• groups are cost-effective, delivering services to more than
  one person at a time;

- groups help socially isolated families meet people and make friends;
- groups tend to build a sense of cohesiveness amongst their members;
- groups provide opportunities for individuals to share their views with others, and learn from others;
- groups build empathy, by encouraging parents to listen to, and respond to, the needs and concerns of others;
- groups can provide appropriate role models;
- groups can provide parents with support and the opportunity to 'network';
- the group process can be powerful in terms of developing self-confidence and self-esteem.

A number of voluntary organisations have been important in the development and promotion of the group approach to parenting education. The three most influential on a country-wide basis are Parent Network, Exploring Parenthood and the Family Caring Trust. Parent Network has its own network of some 30 local Parent-Link organisations which deliver courses through their trained co-ordinators; Exploring Parenthood, based on a psychodynamic approach to parenting education, runs workshops for parents and trains professionals in group work techniques; the Family Caring Trust, drawing eclectically on a number of theoretical backgrounds, has developed a range of programmes which are promoted through existing national and community networks.

Other stimuli have also contributed to the growth of the group approach to parenting education in this country. Professionals, such as health visitors and other health personnel, clinical psychologists and therapists and educational psychologists, have found their resources more and more stretched in recent years. Thus, perhaps for rather more pragmatic reasons, have moved to the use of a group approach in order, primarily, to meet the needs of more families in a more effective way. From another direction has come the increase in schemes which help to promote the involvement of parents in their children's learning through schools and pre-school organisations. In many instances this has led to the introduction of workshops and courses which are overtly and explicitly aimed at helping parents with their parenting tasks. This is over and above the beneficial effects such involvement may have for parents in improving their relationships with their children and increasing the interest they take in their children's learning and development. Community education programmes, such as those developed by the Open University, have had a great influence on the promotion of the group learning method. This will be extended further by their new Parents and Under-8s course, the first part of which is to be launched in 1996. The work of family centres and other family support organisations has also been important in the development of group programmes to meet the expressed needs of parents attending this form of provision. Where such programmes of work are based on the more formal, replicable approach which this survey is specifically about, such as, for example, at The Parents' Centre in Rugby, then it is included. There is, though, a range of other valuable parent group work which falls outside the remit of this study, because of its less formal, possibly more responsive, approach. Examples are the work of Family Service Units, Parents & Co in the London Borough of Camden, 45 Cope Street in Nottingham, the Radford Shared Care Project, family centres, combined centres and family support centres run by the NSPCC and other agencies.

In addition to the reasons often cited for the movement away from the view that parenting can only be 'caught not taught', it is necessary to acknowledge the level of 'moral panic' in this country about the growth in crime and delinquent behaviour, and the blame which is sometimes attached to parents for this phenomenon. A high profile report by Utting and others (1993) proposed a clear link between crime and poor child rearing practices and called, amongst other measures, for an increase in the availability of parenting education. This view is underpinned by the findings of Patterson and colleagues at the Oregon Social Learning Centre (see, for example, Patterson and Narrett, 1990) which points to the value of parent education in reducing subsequent delinquency in children.

Despite the recognition that what in the past tended to be seen as appropriate only for families whose children displayed behaviour problems is now recognised as useful as a preventative measure for 'normal' families, we are still far from having a structured, thought-out approach to the provision of parenting education in the UK. The majority of parents are expected to have an instinctual knowledge of parenting and asking for help still tends to be perceived as failing in the job.

Theoretical frameworks for parenting programmes

As already noted, many of the parenting programmes now available in Britain were developed from earlier work in the USA, and many have adopted, eclectically, aspects of some or all of these theories. The main theoretical traditions which have been influential in the development of parenting programmes are: transactional analysis, humanistic theories (incorporating the work of Carl Rogers), psychodynamic theories, family systems theories, social learning/behavioural theories and the Adlerian approach. The following are brief descriptions of the main theoretical traditions:

Transactional analysis

Transactional analysis (TA) focuses on relationships between people. The theory outlines several processes that are important to personality development and transactions between people. The concept of 'strokes' (or recognition) is basic to the understanding of how and why people relate to each other. Strokes are both conditional (given to people for doing) and unconditional (given to people for being). Each person needs a balance of doing and being strokes to feel good about himself or herself and about other people. In the context of parenting, the way in which parents stroke a child defines, in large part, his or her basic life position, which in turn embodies his or her feelings about self and the world outside self. There are both traditional approaches (Berne, 1964, 1973) and developmental approaches to TA.

The behavioural approach

The behavioural approach focuses on observable and measurable behaviours, that is, any observable and external response. It is also based on the assumption that the overt behaviour of a person can be controlled through the systematic application of social learning theory principles. In the context of parenting education, the model assumes that the application of social learning theory principles is itself a learnable skill, and that parents can be instructed in methods of encouraging desired behaviour in their children and discouraging undesired behaviour.

Humanistic theories

The work of Carl Rogers (1951, 1961) has been influential on parenting programmes. This approach stresses the importance of empathy and *intersubjectivity* in the definition and resolution of emotional and interpersonal problems. The work of Rogers was developed by Thomas Gordon (1975) into a structured programme Parent Effectiveness Training (PET). The emphasis of the training focuses on learning *human relations* strategies that include the use of active listening, sending '*I-messages*' and a '*win-win*' method of resolving conflicts involving *negotiation of a solution satisfactory* to both child and parents.

Psychodynamic theories

Only one programme in the survey used this approach, described by the founder of Exploring Parenthood (Schmidt Neven, 1990) as follows: 'a framework which acknowledges the existence of the unconscious, of an inner world of our dreams and fantasy, which also attributes importance to the very earliest experience of a child's life and development and its effect on later life and which helps us to understand the tension and interplay between the inner and the outer world. It is the psychodynamic framework which provides the link or bridge between our individual and inner world perceptions, our experiences in the family, the way we relate to the surrounding networks and groups in our community and the way we try to integrate societal changes and factors which are beyond our immediate control.'

Family systems theories

This approach arises out of the theory and practice of family therapy. Considerable emphasis is placed on the importance of the individual's understanding of his or her own behaviour and that of others. For example, the interpretation of a child's behaviour in terms of a problem in the family, a problem at school etc. Intervention focuses on the interactional system, for example, relationships in the family, which appear to be the major location of the problem.

Adlerian theory

This approach stems from the writings of Adler (1927, 1930) and has been developed and articulated by Dreikurs and Soltz (1964) and Dinkmeyer and McKay (1976) who developed a highly structured programme Systematic Training for Effective Parenting (STEP). The goals of this approach include helping parents to understand children, to learn how they think and to comprehend the reasons or motives for their behaviour.

The present study

There have been no previous surveys of this type of programme in the UK. One recent study of parenting programmes (Cocks, 1994) focused only on those programmes with involvement by educational psychologists. Another survey of programmes in Ireland (Rylands, 1995) set out, rather as this study did for the UK, to explore needs and current provision in this field and to lay the foundations of a database of parenting programme activities in Ireland.

The aim of the study which led to this book was to explore the range and spread of group-based parenting programmes in the UK; to examine them and analyse them in terms of who they are for, who has access to them, who provides them, their aims and objectives, their content, methods and overall approach, who facilitates the groups and what training staff receive to do this. Answers to a range of questions were sought:

- What group-based parent education schemes are currently in operation in the UK?
- Which organisations are involved in their delivery?
- What is their theoretical base?
- What are their aims and objectives?
- What value base do programmes have?
- What skills are thought to be important for parents?
- Can such skills be taught?
- If so, does the effect last?
- What is the demand for such courses?
- Which parents are courses aimed at? Are they relevant to all ethnic and cultural groups?
- Are courses open access, or by referral? If they are open access, how truly accessible are they?
- What claims do programmes make for success? Is this based on formal evaluation or on anecdotal evidence?
- Which professionals and volunteers are working with parents in these schemes?
- What training do they have?

The methodology included a period of information gathering (July 1994 to January 1995) which involved making contact with known programme providers; calling for information through various professional organisations; sending out a questionnaire; scrutinising programme materials, reports and evaluation studies; meeting with programme providers, researchers and other experts in the field; assessment and analysis of the information gathered. Completed questionnaires were received from 51 respondents, representing 38 different programmes. Between January and March 1995 visits were made to 12 programmes in operation, which provided the opportunity to talk with facilitators, with parents who had attended the courses, and usually to observe a course session in progress. These visits proved invaluable in acquiring background information and in gaining some understanding of the processes at work in the delivery of these programmes. A seminar was held for about 60 people, most of whom were closely connected with the development and delivery of programmes. This proved to be an important event, in that it provided a forum not hitherto available for promoting contact and discussion amongst those involved in this area of work. It was also a most useful way of highlighting the issues which were seen to be important.

So, having set the scene, forthcoming chapters describe some of the findings of the survey. Chapter 2 describes the 'map' uncovered by the survey: the range of programmes and who they are for, the demand for such activities, and their availability and accessibility. Chapters 3, 4 and 5 consider a number of aspects of parenting programmes in practice, looking at: the main players in the field, facilitators and leaders of groups, and how they are being trained and supported; the theoretical base and value base of programmes; some assessment and analysis of courses' objectives, methods, content and materials. The question of the effectiveness of parent education programmes is addressed in Chapter 6; Chapter 7 suggests a possible framework for evaluation. The book concludes with a summary and discussion of the main issues thrown up by the study, with some thoughts on possible ways forward in this field of group-based parenting programmes. Appendix I provides a profile of each programme included in the survey, and Appendix II summarises 15 programme evaluation reports. Appendix III lists a number of organisations working in this field.

2. Parenting programmes in the UK

This chapter describes some of the general findings of the survey which led to the writing of this book. The range of programmes is described; the availability and accessibility of these programmes is discussed; and some estimate of the demand for such programmes is offered.

The range of group-based programmes

This book draws on the information collected about 38 different group-based programmes which have the explicit aim of helping parents improve their parenting skills and family relationships, and which are currently in use in the UK (see Appendix I). The total number of different programmes is, in fact, certainly greater than this. For example, organisations such as the Family Caring Trust, Parent Network and the Family Nurturing Network have each developed a range of programmes, all with a different focus or intended for parents with children of different ages. In addition, it is certain that this survey has not been able, in the time available, to discover every single programme in existence. Initiatives are developing all the time in what is becoming a fast-growing field. Moreover, those programmes which fall only just outside the survey's boundaries have not been included.

Later chapters will explore in more detail the approaches and methods used by these programmes, but at this stage and for the purposes of representing them under two main broad headings (Table 4) they are shown as those which focus primarily on changing children's behaviour (a 'behavioural' approach) and those which mainly address interpersonal relationships within the family (a 'relationships' approach). This classification is not intended to suggest that each programme relies *only* on one or

19

other of these approaches many use both, but the main emphasis is likely to be on one or the other.

Table 4:   Parenting programmes, classified according to their main focus

'Behavioural' programmes	*'Relationships' programmes*
ABC of Behaviour	Black Parents Talking
Asperger Syndrome Parents	Effective Parenting (Barnet &
Coping with Kids	Herts)
(Kidderminster)	Family Caring Trust
Coping with Kids [Assertive	Family Nurturing Network
Discipline]	Help! I'm a parent
Day Group Programme	Mellow Parenting
(Swindon)	NEWPIN
Effective Parenting (Cheshire)	Parents and Under Eights [OU]
Everyday Problems in	Parent Effectiveness Training
Childhood [EPIC]	[PET]
Goal Planning Course (Haringey)	Parent Network
Handling Children's Behaviour	Parenthood Group [YOIs]
Living with Teenagers (Surrey)	Parenting Course (Stockport)
Managing Difficult Children	Parents against crime
Parent Workshops (Southwark)	Parents 'n' Kids
Positive Parenting (Durham)	Parentwise (Birmingham)
Promoting Positive Parenting	Parentwise (Plymouth)
Seven Supertactics for	Parent-Infant Network [PIPPIN]
Superparents	Positive Parenting Packs
The Parents & Children Series	(Portsmouth)
Toddler Taming/Behaviour	Special Parenting Programme
Management	Systematic Training for
Working with Parents for	Effective Parenting [STEP]
Change	

The particular characteristics and operation of all 38 programmes are summarised in Appendix I, but at this point some examples are given in order to illustrate the range of different approaches. Four of the 'behavioural' approach programmes and four of the 'relationships' type are described.

ABC of Behaviour

This programme was developed by an educational psychologist who has been working in Surrey for about 12 years. Workshops and five-session courses have been running in association with schools in the county since 1982. The ABC booklet which accompanies the course explains the behavioural approach in straightforward language with amusing illustrations. It offers examples of problems which many parents encounter and gives clear instructions on how to follow and understand the ABC of behaviour (antecedents, behaviour and consequences), so that acceptable behaviour results, and unwanted behaviour decreases. During the course, discussion focuses on parents' own problems and how they may be solved by the ABC approach. There is much emphasis on the use of praise for desired behaviour, rather than criticism of unwanted behaviour. Health visitors and school nurses have been trained to run groups using the ABC method.

Handling Children's Behaviour

This programme was developed and a publication written by a social worker working in child guidance in the West Midlands. There is no parents' handbook to accompany the course, although parts of the publication can be used as handouts at the different sessions. The leaders' guide has been published by NCH Action for Children and the programme is widely used in family centres and under-5s centres in Coventry, Birmingham, Warwickshire and many other parts of the country. Adaptations have also been made for use with parents of children with special needs. The course usually consists of ten weekly sessions of two hours duration. 'Homework' in the form of keeping records and practising the behaviour management skills discussed in the session is a feature of this programme, as of many others based on behavioural principles. The sessions cover: types of behaviour; parents and children; rules; consequences and consistency; reinforcing behaviour; recording wanted behaviour; play; finding solutions; relaxation; problem solving using the principles learned in the course.

The Parents and Children Series

This is a rather different approach aimed at helping parents to understand how their own behaviour impacts on their children, using a series of very short video vignettes depicting instances of family interaction. The group discussion about each video scene then focuses on comments about the way in which parents reacted, and suggestions about more positive ways of reacting to particular situations. The 'corrected' version of the video scene is then shown to the group. The work was developed by clinical psychologist Carolyn Webster-Stratton in Seattle,

USA. It was originally intended for use with referred families whose children have severe behaviour difficulties, but trials have taken place at the Maudsley Hospital in London using the method with groups of self-referred parents. The video scenarios have now been dubbed with an English (as opposed to American) accent, and there are plans to develop a whole new version more suited to use with families in the UK.

Coping with Kids

This programme is the British adaptation of Lee Canter's *Assertive Discipline for Parents,* published in the USA in 1985. It consists of three two-hour sessions which focus on the skills of staying calm, taking control and enjoying family life. The materials and activities have been adapted to meet the needs of parents living in deprived city areas in the UK as well as parents from more affluent backgrounds. Workshops have been run in the county of Avon since 1992, based in various centres including schools, health clinics, social services department day nurseries, church and community centres. The aim of the programme is to effect initial changes within the family system, through increasing parents' skills, confidence and self-esteem.

Family Caring Trust

The parenting programmes developed and published by this organisation based in Northern Ireland are described as easy-to-run, flexible, self-help, six- to eight-week courses for small groups of parents. The four main programmes are Basic Parenting; Teen Parenting; Parent Assertiveness; Parenting and Sex. A programme for parents of babies and young children has recently been added to the range. Each has a parents' handbook and a leader's guide. There are instructions for each session, including audio or videotapes presenting typical family situations. The overall objectives of these programmes are to enable parents to communicate better with their children, and to develop a growing sense of self-responsibility in their children. Courses are organised through schools, health visitors, churches and other community organisations.

Family Nurturing Network

The Nurturing Programme is a course for groups of parents and their children (aged four to 12 years) together, many of whom may have multiple problems in their lives. It aims to promote positive parenting and nurturing skills throughout the whole family and to prevent and reduce physical and emotional abuse and neglect. The programme consists of 15 weekly sessions, with children's and adults' groups separately tackling similar topics (such as anger; praise; power; time-out; self-esteem) at their appropriate levels. The programme was developed by Stephen Bavolek at the Family Resource Centre, Utah, USA and is in use in Oxford by the Family Nurturing Network, where some modifications have been made to the length and structure of some programmes to make them more appropriate for British families.

Parent-Infant Network (PIPPIN)

PIPPIN developed from Parent Network, and started as a separate organisation in 1991. It is a structured, preventative education and support programme for couples which complements traditional antenatal and parentcraft classes. Its aim is to support the development of positive early family and parent-child relationships. PIPPIN groups begin around the fourth month of pregnancy, and there are four phases: Great Expectations, Review, Home Visit and Life after Birth. These comprise a total of 17 sessions, plus the home visit which takes place as soon as possible after the birth. The focus throughout is on emotional support, communication and problem-solving skills, and sensitivity to the infant as a person. Specially designed (but not published) parent notes are given to participants to enable them to build on ideas and skills between sessions. PIPPIN started in the Home Counties and training of facilitators is allowing expansion of the number of groups, both on a freelance basis and within the NHS.

Parents and Under-8s (Open University)

The Open University has 17 years of experience of developing courses on parenting and childcare (for example, The Preschool Years, The First Years of Life and Parents and Teenagers). The OU is currently working in partnership with a wide range of agencies and with national early years education and childcare networks to develop a major new parenting education programme, Parents and Under-8s. Using a mixture of supported open learning and training and support for group leaders, the OU anticipates that this programme will reach at least 50,000 parents within the first five years. The course will consist of six modules[*], the first of which will be available in Spring 1996: Confident Parents, Confident Children; Understanding Development; Supporting Parents and Children; Parents and Children within the Family; Parents and Children in the Community; Parents, Children and Schools. The ten topics to be included in the first module are: Growing together; Wanting the best; Building children's self-esteem; Valuing families; Parents are people first; The job of parenting; Learning from experience; Is there a handbook?; Children's rights; Confident parenting. There will also be a group leader's pack and an assessment pack. Each module will be built round a highly illustrated study book containing short, self-contained topics, allowing flexibility for group learning. The book will be supported by audiotapes and a personal workbook.

These few descriptions of selected programmes have, hopefully, given a flavour of the range of approaches used in these courses. Further aspects of them will be considered in forthcoming sections of the book.

Geographical spread

Several of the programmes listed in Table 4 have been allocated a geographical location. This generally indicates the locality in which the programme was first developed and often where it is still primarily in use. Only two organisations – Parent Network and the Family Caring Trust have a country-wide coverage which is achieved by these two organisations in very different ways. Parent Network operates through a number of geographically spread local Parent-Link organisations, each with its own trained co-ordinators. The Family Caring Trust has its base in Newry, Northern Ireland and distributes the materials through existing networks and community organisations such as churches and schools, and through health visitors and other professionals.

A number of programmes, for example, the Family Nurturing Network, Parent Effectiveness Training (PET), Systematic Training for Effective Parenting (STEP) and the Parents and Children Series, were developed in the United States of America and are quite widely used there. Some programmes are also

---

*   There is some uncertainty as to whether the full programme can be completed as planned.

relatively common in Australia. However, it would seem that, so far, extensive networks for these programmes have not yet developed in this country.

Who are the programmes intended for?

It would appear from the literature that there has been little systematic attempt to match the development of parenting pro- grammes with the particular characteristics and needs of dif- ferent parents. Parents do not constitute a uniform group with common needs: family forms and cultures vary widely, family circumstances are very different, and parents' needs change over time. A young parent suffering from postnatal depression will have needs which are very different from those of a parent trying to cope with the demands of a teenager. In addition to these varying needs of different groups, parents also vary in the way they are able to make use of particular methods and tech- niques, to grasp concepts and to make use of written material. These two variables of need and acceptability are interlinked, and also have to be considered when looking at what motivates parents to attend group programmes. Another way, then, of attempting to classify the programmes described in this report is according to the needs of the parents to whom the pro- grammes are primarily offered. Three main groups of parents involved in group parenting programmes present themselves:

- Parents who want to do a 'good enough' job of parenting
- Parents whose children have behaviour problems, in either the 'normal' range (which any child might be expected to display) or 'severe' range (which may require clinical inter- vention)
- Parents with multiple problems and very low self-esteem.

Table 5 shows how the programmes can be divided, using this classification.

Although each developmental period can bring its own stresses and strains for parents, two particularly testing peri- ods are during the transition from toddler to young child, and again from child to young adult – the period of adolescence. So another way of classifying which parents the programmes are intended for is to consider the age of their children. In fact, the majority of programmes described in this book are intended primarily for parents of young children, usually under five or under eight. For some parents though, when their children are

Table 5:   Parenting programmes, classified according to their main clientele

- **Parents who want to do a 'good enough' job of parenting**

  Black Parents Talking
  Effective Parenting (Hartley-Brewer/Hills)
  Family Caring Trust
  Help! I'm a parent
  Living with Teenagers (Surrey)
  Parents and Under Eights (OU)
  Parent Effectiveness Training (PET)Parenthood Group (YOIs)
  Parent–Infant Network (PIPPIN)
  Parents 'n' Kids
  Parent Network
  Parentwise (Birmingham)
  Parentwise (Plymouth)
  Positive Parenting Packs (Portsmouth)
  Systematic Training for Effective Parenting (STEP)

- **Parents whose children have behaviour problems**
  – within the 'normal' range

  ABC of Behaviour
  Coping with Kids (Assertive Discipline)
  Coping with Kids (Kidderminster)
  Effective Parenting (Cheshire)
  Everyday Problems in Childhood (EPIC)
  Goal Planning Course (Haringey)
  Handling Children's Behaviour
  Managing Difficult Children
  Parenting Course (Stockport)
  Parents against crime
  Parent Workshops (Southwark)
  Positive Parenting (Durham)
  Promoting Positive Parenting
  Seven Supertactics for Superparents
  Toddler Taming/Behaviour Management
  Working with Parents for Change

  – within the 'severe' range

  Day Group Programme (Swindon)
  Parents of children with Asperger Syndrome
  The Parents and Children Series

- **Parents with multiple problems and very low self-esteem**

  Family Nurturing Network
  Mellow Parenting
  NEWPIN
  Special Parenting Programme

teenagers, outside support and help again become necessary, and some programmes specifically for parents of adolescents are being developed. Examples are Living with Teenagers (developed by Sonya Hinton in Guildford, Surrey), Living with Teenagers (Parent Network) and What can the parent of a teenager do? (Family Caring Trust).

Availability and accessibility

The programmes in the first group of Table 5 (those which are primarily for parents who want to do a 'good enough' job of parenting) tend to adopt a completely open access approach – any parent may attend. This is particularly true of programmes such as those developed by the Family Caring Trust, Parent Network, PIPPIN, Parent Effectiveness Training and Systematic Training for Effective Parenting. However, even within these relatively generalised programmes, parents will only have the choice of attending if they live in a locality where a scheme is running. Moreover, whether or not parents get to hear about these programmes is also likely to be fairly hit and miss, and dependent on the extent to which parents are integrated into existing networks through which they might hear about forthcoming courses. Effective Parenting (Hartley-Brewer and Hills), for example, is available to parents whose children are attending particular schools in a few local education authorities through which the programme is offered; educational psychologists in Surrey offering the ABC of Behaviour programme work through a number of nursery, primary and secondary schools in the Guildford area; the various modules of Parentwise (Plymouth) are available on an open access basis, but only to those parents living within a quite small area of Devonport.

A measure of the accessibility of a support service must include factors other than merely its geographical location. To be truly accessible, parenting programmes must be affordable, held in appropriate premises, at an appropriate time of day and, for parents of young children, need to be accompanied by crèche facilities. So far as cost to participants is concerned, those programmes which are funded by statutory agencies such as education or health do not charge fees to participants. There are some examples where participants pay a token sum, sometimes on a voluntary basis, to cover refreshments. Independent programmes, such as Parent-Link and Family Caring Trust, have generally to be self-supporting and parents pay a fee. For Parent-Link courses, this is usually between £60 and £70 for a 12-session course, although subsidies from a centrally held fund are sometimes available for parents who cannot afford the full fee. There are also examples of Parent-Link putting on courses for social services departments, and as part of adult community education programmes, in which case costs may be paid by the statutory agency. The Family Caring Trust parents' handbooks cost about £5 per copy and it is recommended that each participant buys one. A small additional fee may be charged to cover the cost of hiring a room and refreshments. Facilitators do not generally take a fee. PIPPIN operates a sliding scale of fees, up to a maximum of £50 per person. (All costs quoted are correct at the time of publication.)

So far as premises are concerned, a wide range of local community facilities are used for parenting courses, some more suitable than others in terms of their comfort and ambience. Again, the independent programmes differ in that very often groups meet in the homes of facilitators. While this may provide a warm, comfortable and welcoming environment, the idea of going into someone else's private domain may be threatening to some parents. Finding the ideal time of day for courses can also be a problem. Daytime courses cannot always attract fathers, and evening courses can make it difficult for both parents to attend at the same time. Where young children are involved, the provision of a crèche or other form of child care is generally seen to be essential to the success of a programme.

Over and above these practical considerations of accessibility, programmes need to be acceptable to parents. Parents may need to be reassured that to attend such a programme will not lead to a label of 'failed parent', that they are not being blamed for things going wrong, and that it is alright to acknowledge problems, to ask for advice or merely to receive approval of their parenting skills and style. Parents with a poor educational experience themselves, or who have learning disabilities, may need to know that they will be able to cope with the demands of a course. Black and minority ethnic group parents may wonder about the relevance of such a course to them, where value systems may be quite different from those of course presenters and the majority of participants. Fathers may resist attending something which they may see as women's work.

Several programmes use more than one method for recruiting their participants. The majority of respondents to this survey (69 per cent) reported that their programmes were open access, but at the same time some participants might be referred by social services or other agencies such as health visitors. Other programmes might use an open invitation approach, but within a group of parents who are already attending a facility such as a family centre. For some programmes, a more limited open access approach is offered to parents who are already attending a particular support or therapeutic facility on a referred basis, such as child guidance clinics, family centres or NEWPIN centres.

Meeting parents' needs

Any consideration of accessibility and availability should include some discussion about the primary expressed motivation of parents to attend such programmes. Motivation emanates from need, and the needs of each and every parent may be very different. Quotations from just four parents who attended a course illustrate a few of the motivations which parents may display:

'When I first came to the parenting group I was feeling...

'...a bit lost. Feeling useless at times and downtrodden.'

'...out on a limb with low self-esteem, feeling a failure as a parent of a strong-willed child.'

'...depressed and unhappy at the way I was playing the role of motherhood.'

'...that the group would be a good opportunity to expand my horizons in parenting.'

Other reasons which parents gave for attending were to obtain information and advice from someone they perceive as an expert; to gain reinforcement for the way in which they were parenting and to meet other people with children of a similar age.

Parent education in the USA has been described as being characterised by a 'supermarket' approach, making its wares known and inviting all parents to participate. The results of this present survey indicate that this is not what is happening in the UK. Many of the programmes described here seem to have specific parent audiences in mind, and, therefore, target specific groups of parents, or agencies and organisations where these parents are likely to be found, or through which they can be contacted.

But does each of the parenting programmes described here meet the needs of all parents who might need or want to attend? That is, as suggested in the proposed principles (see Chapter 1) does each of them reach parents of different social and economic classes, of different educational levels, of different ethnic groups and both fathers and mothers? In other words, is there equality of access to all the programmes for all these groups? Taking each group in turn, the following comments are relevant:

Socioeconomic group

The two most widespread programmes, Parent Network and Family Caring Trust, appear to be more available to, and more accessible to, parents who might describe themselves as middle class. This is acknowledged by the two organisations, and was evident during the visits made during the study. However, there are increasingly examples of these programmes being used by a broader cross-section of parents and of their being funded by both social services departments and health agencies. Programmes offered through schools, such as Coping with Kids and Effective Parenting are likely to attract parents from a cross-section of the whole local parent group, while programmes such as the Special Parenting Programme tend to reach parents who are all of low socioeconomic status. Some respondents to the survey suggested that they encouraged the mixing of socioeconomic groups, and that parents found that they had bonds which they did not suspect:

> 'Basically, everyone has a story to tell – problems with children are a great leveller!'

Different educational levels

Evidence from facilitators indicates that quite frequently prepared or published material has to be adapted to meet the needs of parents who are not comfortable with the written word, or who find relatively sophisticated concepts difficult to grasp. Fewer written exercises may have to be used, more time given to some aspects or topics, and a generally more informal approach adopted. There are other examples too, such as that of the health visitor who, using the frameworks of two or three published programmes, has developed an even more eclectic programme of her own to meet specific local needs. The parent teaching methods developed by McGaw (1993, 1994, 1995) with parents with learning disabilities are of particular interest. The group approach complements home teaching, using specially developed materials.

Different cultural and ethnic groups

Most parent education programmes derive from white, middle class goals and values, not always recognising different attitudes to child rearing practices. Only one of the programmes, Black Families Talking, appeared to directly address the specific support and information needs of black parents. Some others acknowledged the need to adapt materials on some occasions, making sure that they could offer appropriate examples of parenting or suggest strategies which supported the principles of various cultures. Others felt that individual parents could work towards their own goals, so that no single cultural approach need be dominant. There is some evidence to indicate, however, that the majority of people who attend these programmes are white, and Baginsky (1993) in an evaluation of a Parent-Link programme in a London borough, drew attention to the need and demand for more courses for specific groups of parents, such as African-Caribbean and Asian parents.

Fathers and mothers

There was evidence from a number of sources that few fathers attended the majority of these parenting programmes. Some all-mother groups actually felt that they preferred it that way, and so little effort was made to recruit fathers. In other cases, one parent or the other was able to attend, usually for practical baby-sitting reasons. Except for PIPPIN, which is a programme specifically designed for couples, it appeared to be comparatively rare for both parents to attend at the same time. Programme facilitators encouraged parents to discuss the course content with partners so that a consistent approach could be adopted at home. Some respondents reported addressing male and female roles and responsibilities, which sometimes raised difficulties over the attitudes of male partners.

Overall, many programmes do appear to make explicit their belief that there is no blueprint for parenting, and that a variety of parenting styles must be recognised and respected. However, although many programme authors and facilitators are attempting to meet the needs of a wide range of parents (within the group for whom the programme is primarily intended), there are indications that some of the more widely available programmes (such as Parent Network and Family Caring Trust) are attracting mainly white, middle class women. Few participants are male, black or from lower socioeconomic groups.

On the other hand, there is the argument that each and every programme should *not* be trying to meet the needs of all parents. Is it, perhaps, better to 'let a thousand flowers bloom' in order to ensure that there is a range of programmes into which parents can slot in order to meet their needs at different times in their parenting lives?

Perhaps one of the most exciting developments for potentially massively increasing the access of all parents to help with parenting is the Parents and Under-8s programme being developed by the Open University. The success of the OU's approach with their earlier community education programmes, and their determination to meet the needs of many more parents in a flexible way with this new programme, is opportune.

The demand for parenting programmes

There has undoubtedly been a considerable expansion in recent years in the number of published course materials used in parenting education. This survey has also found that, in addition to published materials, there has been a growth in small-scale unpublished programmes. It would seem that there is also increased interest in such approaches, both from professionals and para-professionals delivering the courses, from agencies funding them, and from parents participating in such programmes. In particular, the role of statutory organisations (health, education and social services) appears to have increased. Two questions present themselves in this connection: why are professionals increasingly adopting the view that parenting programmes are important, especially for particular groups of parents? And secondly, what is it that motivates some parents, but not others, to ask for such help or to take up offers of such help? Both of these questions are complex, but can perhaps be partially answered by referring back to the points made in Chapter 1 about the particular pressures on parents today, and the concerns shown in some quarters about the quality of parenting and its effects on children and young people and, indeed, on the next generation of parents.

So far as the evidence from this study shows, there would appear to be a certain amount of mismatch between what professionals and others think that parents need and parents' own uptake of programmes designed to meet that need. Although just over half the respondents to the survey reported that they had a waiting list, 14 per cent had no waiting list, and others reported that the situation varied in different areas so that it was not easy to generalise. Interestingly, there was also some anecdotal evidence that advertised courses had to be cancelled because of lack of interest. One respondent (a professional) cited a possible reason for this:

> 'In the UK it's a matter of educating parents that it's OK to go [on parenting courses]'

or, as a seminar delegate put it,

> 'We need to "normalise" the idea of attending parenting courses.'

In a recent survey of parenting and parents' needs, carried out by Exploring Parenthood through Sainsbury's magazine (Katz, 1994) over 60 per cent of the 14,000 parent respondents said that they would welcome parenting skills training if it were available. This would appear to indicate a fairly strong call for help of this kind, amongst this particular readership at least. A further survey of parent support services (Crisp, 1994) concluded that 'few services are available for parents who wish to develop better parenting skills in an atmosphere which does not pre-judge some failure.' A small scale survey undertaken by the Office of Population Censuses and Surveys (Roberts, 1995) found that one-fifth of parents in the survey said that they had sought outside help for a problem with a child.

The present survey found that about 60 per cent of respondents running programmes reported heavy demand:

> 'Can't keep up with demand!' (Handling Children's Behaviour)

> 'Receiving enquiries all the time.' (Parentwise, Birmingham)

> 'Very high [demand] – could easily double the number of groups if we had the funding.' (Centre for Fun and Families).

These were typical of these responses. Others, however, indicated that, although the potential for expansion was there, it was not always demonstrated by parents queuing up to attend. This was said to be particularly so for programmes which are run through schools, where recruitment methods had to be carefully selected. A note sent home to parents via pupils was not, for example, very effective. There was general agreement that 'word of mouth' was the best method of encouraging people to commit themselves to attending a programme, very often through someone who had already been on a previous course. Some group leaders and facilitators recommend holding an open information meeting initially in order to ensure that potential participants are well aware of what is on offer and its suitability for their particular needs. One programme organiser found that offering incentives, such as free raffle tickets, where the draw would be made at the end of each session, was a useful tactic.

Interestingly, what also emerged from this study was a large number of reported requests for training in the use of parenting programmes. Indeed, lack of trained facilitators was cited as one of the reasons for slow growth and expansion of a programme. There was also a general feeling that professionals such as health visitors felt under-trained and unsupported in this area of work and were therefore sometimes hesitant to introduce it, despite being convinced of its benefits and of their role as parent educators.

So far as the extent and spread of parenting programmes across Britain is concerned, it has not been possible through this survey to arrive at an accurate picture. As already indicated, many of the programmes are relatively small scale and local in delivery, reaching fewer than 100 parents per year. Another cluster of two or three programmes reported that they reached 200-300 parents per year. Parent Network, through its 30 Parent-Link organisations, reaches around 2,000 parents per year, and the Family Caring Trust estimates that at least 20,000 parents per year are reached by its range of programmes. Provision is patchy, though, and often dependent on the interest of particular individuals or organisations: for example, a concerted effort to set up as many Family Caring Trust programmes as possible in a rural area of North Yorkshire. This initiative is being funded by a wide range of statutory and voluntary bodies and churches over a three-year period. A further example of a high level of Parent-Link activity is the county of Devon where there is a strong and active Devon Parent Network, which has its own family centre, in addition to running parenting programmes.

Through a process of estimation it is possible to conclude that, overall, the type of parenting programmes described in this survey may be reaching some 28,000 parents per year in the UK. Assuming that the 12 million or so parents of dependent children might attend this type of programme only once during the 20 years or so which they spend bringing up their children, this represents an approximate attendance rate of about four per cent at the present time. Adding in the less formal group work undertaken by family centres and other family support projects it would perhaps be fair to double this figure, so that perhaps overall such approaches are reaching around 60,000 parents per year, or eight per cent of eligible parents.

The overall impression gained during work on this project was that parent education generally, and group-based parenting programmes in particular, are acquiring an increasingly high profile in the UK. It is a rapidly growing and changing field in which development and innovation are making it more and more likely that tomorrow's parents will have the opportunity to attend such programmes, and many will feel comfortable doing so.

3. Who provides parenting programmes?

The aim of this chapter is to paint a picture of the way in which group-based parenting programmes are being promoted in the UK: that is, the organisations and individuals involved, the group leaders and facilitators, and the training and support available to them.

The agencies involved

This study has highlighted the wide range of organisations and individuals involved in the delivery of parenting education in the UK, and also in the financial support of this work. Statutory health and welfare organisations, as well as voluntary organisations, are increasingly advocating parenting education as part of their family support strategies, for a variety of reasons. Almost two-thirds of the programmes contacted during the survey were operated by statutory organisations, and over two-thirds of the total received the majority of their funding from statutory organisations, principally health authorities or trusts, local education authorities or social services departments. All of the following were involved to some extent in either organising or funding (or both) group parenting programmes:

- Local education authorities, via educational psychology services, schools and pre-school services, parent partnership programmes.
- Health authorities, health trusts and community health units, child guidance units.
- Social services departments (mainly nurseries and family centres).
- Voluntary organisations.
- Churches and other faith groups.
- Home Office (via Young Offender Institutions and prisons).

- Academic institutions.
- Private businesses (usually for marketing and dissemination).

Most support appears to come at present from local education authorities and health authorities. Twenty seven per cent of the questionnaire responses indicated that education departments were involved in operating the programme, and 24 per cent that health authorities were similarly involved. Twelve per cent indicated that financial support was received from social services departments. Additionally, through their financial support for voluntary organisations it is likely that the statutory sector is indirectly funding an even greater proportion of these programmes.

Why statutory services?

The reasons that statutory services have become involved in this method of delivery of parenting support are multiple, and vary for different agencies. In the case of educational psychologists, for example, there is evidence that growing numbers of referrals have provided the motivation to search for effective ways to help parents who are experiencing behavioural problems with their children, or who are at risk of doing so. Requests for help are received from head teachers, health visitors, general practitioners, social workers and directly from parents themselves. The authors of the programme Working with Parents for Change suggest that certain common factors are evident in children whose behaviour gives cause for concern, or who are referred to the psychological service. They report that parents say that they feel insecure in the parenting role, and may have a poor understanding of their children's emotional, educational and social needs. Children may then arrive at nursery school or primary school lacking in maturity and social skills, may exhibit uninhibited behaviour, be unable to accept direction and have difficulty in responding appropriately to others. For some, although the nursery or school experience may resolve most of these problems in the school setting, difficulties may still exist at home. Edwards and Townsend (1993), both educational psychologists in Strathclyde, Scotland, suggest that:

> 'Of the options available, group work with parents seems to have great potential in that it can provide information and advice but, more importantly, can provide a supportive setting in which

parents can develop their skills. In order to meet the needs of such families, such groups would benefit from being set up within the local community, being located in the pre-5 centre or primary school, and making use of key trained staff as group leaders.'(Working with Parents for Change, Handbook, p.6)

In the case of health visitors and other community health workers, there appear to be a variety of reasons for their involvement. They are in touch with families with young children and recognise parents' needs for friendship, peer support, information and general skills of parenting, as well as the more traditional role in supporting parents with nutrition, health issues, safety, weaning, and so on, often on a one-to-one basis. Reorganisation, cuts in services and changes in ways of working are putting increasing pressures on health visitors, so that they may perceive a group method as a more efficient way of offering support to a greater number of families. An alternative motivation for parent education (not just group-based methods but applicable to these) is suggested by Jeanette Edwards (1995), in a study based on two localities in the Greater Manchester area. She proposes that, 'in the face of burgeoning poverty and contracting spheres of influence', health and social service workers perceive parenting skills as a body of knowledge which they can teach, thus providing a strategy for these professionals to improve the lives of the families with whom they work. This activity offers a way for such professionals to actively 'do something' to improve the lives of families, instead of remaining passive and powerless to do anything about the poverty, poor housing and lack of child care and play facilities in the area in which the families live. Edwards is, however, critical of this approach which, as she sees it, lays the blame for most social ills on *mothers* who are perceived as not coping as parents. Professionals, and volunteers, by so doing screen out the effects of wider forms of social and economic disadvantage, and 'deflect responsibility away from men, service providers and the state.'

Social workers providing family support have, since the implementation of the Children Act 1989, given a substantial amount of their time and resources to the investigation of alleged child abuse incidents. This is sometimes at the expense of allocating resources to a more preventative approach of providing families with support services before, rather than after, a crisis occurs. There are examples, though, of funding and support for group parenting programmes, especially for families who are deemed to be at risk of family breakdown. Family centres and children's centres, run either solely by social services departments, or in partnership with other agencies, seem increasingly to be adopting the groupwork approach as an effective way of providing support for families. As noted previously, however, this type of work often tends to be offered in a more flexible way in order to meet the parents' specific needs, and so is not always included in this survey.

The pioneers

It is apparent that the implementation, and sometimes also the development, of a significant number of programmes in the UK is dependent, at least initially, on the interest and enthusiasm of one individual, or a group of individuals. Examples of this include the PIPPIN programme which was developed in collaboration with Parent Network by Mel Parr, who undertook an initial action research programme; and the Parentwise programme in Plymouth which is currently being developed by Peter Jones, a community psychologist who believes that a multi-agency cooperative approach is one which will work in that particular location. Sonya Hinton, an educational psychologist in Surrey was responsible for the development of the ABC of Behaviour approach into a form which could be used with groups of parents located through schools. Hugh Clench, another educational psychologist in the Brighton area developed Everyday Problems in Childhood (EPIC). A social worker in child guidance in the West Midlands, Graham Finch, perceived that an increasing number of parents were approaching the centre seeking help and guidance on managing their children's behaviour. His recognition of the factors common to many of these situations led to the development of a group work approach to address some of the issues identified by families. This resulted in the publication of Handling Children's Behaviour (Finch, 1994). Dr Stephen Scott, a clinical psychologist in London recognised similar needs of families, and explored the use of video-based therapeutic methods with groups of parents, both as treatment for referred families and as a preventative measure with families in which the problems had not yet become too severe. With their programme Effective Parenting, Hartley-Brewer and Hills (1994) recognised the pressures on teachers and schools, both in coping with an increase in non-compliant behaviour of children in school, and requests for help from parents. This programme underwent a pilot stage of development in schools in Barnet and Hertfordshire. A programme well-established in the USA, Bavolek's Nurturing Programme, was taken up by a group of professionals (clinical nurse specialist, health visitor and clinical psychologist) in Oxford who founded the Family Nurturing Network, perceiving this approach as an effective intervention for families with children at risk of physical and emotional abuse and neglect.

The number of examples of separate initiatives described here, and more could be cited, goes some way to explaining why so many of these programmes are at present restricted to local areas. Several, though, appear to be at the stage where they are poised for expansion, provided funding can be found, so this situation could change significantly in the future.

Networking

It is perhaps inaccurate to describe this mushroom-type growth of programmes in the UK over the past few years as *ad hoc*, but it may be relevant to ask questions about learning from others before plunging in. It became evident during this study that people involved in parenting programmes were not always aware of and in touch with other similar work, and would welcome the opportunity to network and make links. The project provided one opportunity to do this, through a well-attended seminar held at the National Children's Bureau during March 1995. This day had several positive outcomes, not the least of which was the opportunity to meet and exchange views with others working in the same field. Appendix I provides contact names, addresses and telephone numbers, as well as descriptions of the different approaches of programmes, so this too may be helpful in encouraging interchange and networking.

A further opportunity to make links has been provided by the establishment in 1994 by members of the British Psychological Society of a national association of psychologists (educational, clinical and community psychologists) known as Promoting Parenting Skills. This group, while not limiting its interest to the group-work method of parenting education, is likely to be influential in its promotion and development, given the number of psychologists who are already working in this way (see Appendix III).

The recently established (June 1995) Parenting Education and Support Forum provides a further opportunity for information exchange and networking between a very wide range of professionals working in a huge variety of ways with parents. Such cross-fertilisation of ideas, despite the variety of approaches and viewpoints from which people come, must be beneficial and will help to refine and consolidate a body of work which has a broadly common purpose – raising the profile of parenting, the support of parents and improvement in children's lives.

One example of the way in which sharing information might have helped one project is suggested by the following comment from the Family Nurturing Network (questionnaire response, 1994):

> 'It is extremely hard work setting up projects from scratch. Perhaps before projects begin they should be given... training re all the basic steps, from Insurance to PAYE. With hindsight, a business manager would have been useful from the beginning but, of course, limited funds made this a difficult decision. One needs the clinical staff to pioneer the work but one can get "overloaded" by having to run a business and carry out the clinical work. National networking would be a great help and save a lot of time.'

Group leaders and facilitators

Education authorities and health authorities alike are becoming more involved with the promotion and implementation of parenting programmes. A review of the individual professionals involved in facilitating the groups confirms this. Although there is a wide range of personnel involved in this way (see Table 6), the two largest groups of professionals emerging from this survey are educational psychologists and health visitors, followed by social workers and teachers. A number of programme authors, though, take the view that parenting should not become too professionalised within their own communities, and parents themselves make more appropriate facilitators – understanding and sharing experiences, helping to create local networks and not 'talking down' to other parents. The two most widely available programmes, Parent Network and Family Caring Trust, especially encourage the evolution of new group leaders from parent participants. This, indeed, is undoubtedly one of the key reasons why these two programmes have multiplied as they have.

The list in Table 6 illustrates the range of professionals and others involved in this type of work with parents and hence reflects a diversity of perspectives, a range of emphases and

Table 6:   Range of professionals and others who facilitate programmes

Care worker
Clinical psychologist
Community worker
Counsellor
Educational psychologist
Family worker
Head teacher
Health visitor
Mental health worker/psychiatric nurse
Midwife
Nursery nurse
Parent
Portage worker
Project staff/leader
School liaison worker
School nurse
Social worker
Social work lecturer/tutor
Staff of various voluntary agencies
Teacher
Volunteers from various backgrounds

different approaches, and different preparation for the role of parent educator. Health visitors, in particular, seem to be increasing their role in this field and becoming important players. In addition to the information gained by the formal replies to the present survey, a good response was also received from a call to health visitors in the field via the Health Visitors Association. Between 30 and 40 health visitors from all parts of the country provided information about their activities in this area. This group of professionals appears to be broadening its role in two ways: first, in extending the traditional parent health education role which emphasises the health and physical care of babies and young children, to include other aspects of parenting – roles, relationships, play and discipline; and second, working with groups of parents rather than the more usual one-to-one approach at home or at clinic visits. Several health visitors had introduced the Family Caring Trust's programmes, and some were then involving parents in leading subsequent groups. Others had developed their own materials, and some had widened existing postnatal groups to include topics of general parenting interest, rather than concentrating on feeding, health and safety as in the past. Several respondents mentioned the promotion of positive parenting, and the aim of building parents' self confidence. There is some evidence from this trawl that, in some areas at least, there is useful inter-agency co-ordination going on, with health visitors running these programmes jointly with schools, or with social workers, or through parent/toddler groups.

The wide involvement of educational psychologists in this area of work has already been noted. Many programmes have been developed, and in some cases published, by educational psychologists as, for example, The ABC of Behaviour and Working with Parents for Change (see Appendix I). Cuts in support services, such as educational psychology in recent years have led professionals to explore other ways of working, and to develop preventative methods which will hopefully help parents to address problems before they become too unmanageable. Clinical psychologists and psychotherapists have also moved into the groupwork method, and some have adapted their approach to work in a preventative way with parents whose children do not have severe behaviour problems, but may be at risk of doing so.

The skills of group leaders and facilitators

The skills required to work with parents are perhaps even more important than professional background. Pugh and others (1994) suggest that facilitators need to:

- be skilled in handling groups:
  - able to provide a supportive learning environment;
  - be clear about their aims and objectives, and the underpinning values of their work;
  - be able to develop strategies for handling sensitive issues and managing conflict;
  - to value what individuals bring to the group.

- be skilled in communicating:
  - be able to facilitate discussion;
  - be able to observe and listen.

- have some counselling skills:
  - enabling participants to become more self-aware, and able to work on their own problems;
  - be able to avoid making judgements about people;

- be self-aware, conscious of their own values and behaviours;
- be able to handle their own emotions;
- be open, honest and approachable;
- have sufficient expertise to feed into the group as appropriate.

This represents a list of basic, general skills which are likely to be required, to some extent at least by all parenting programmes. However, the different aims and objectives and methods of the various programmes will clearly call for somewhat different specialised skills. For example, an educational psychologist leading Coping with Kids groups felt that the most important ability for facilitators was a teaching skill. Another educational psychologist using the ABC of Behaviour approach felt that group work skills and psychologists' skills were the most important. Facilitators of the Family Nurturing Network's more in-depth programme, largely for 'at risk' families, felt that a 'sensitive' and 'accepting' approach, together with an atmosphere of 'optimism' were more appropriate skills for that particular intervention. A Family Caring Trust group leader also felt that 'sensitivity' was vital, as well as enthusiasm for the methods and skills being introduced to parents. Another Family Caring Trust facilitator highlighted the importance of 'listening skills' and also felt that 'it helped to have been a teacher.' The PIPPIN philosophy suggests that facilitators need to develop certain facilitation skills which ensure that parents' groups meet a range of goals, such as increasing self-confidence, providing opportunities for problem solving and decision making, and promoting an atmosphere of mutual aid and support.

The role of group leaders and facilitators

The Leaders' guide from the Family Caring Trust's programme What Can a Parent Do? provides some guidance on the role of leaders. To begin with, the booklet asserts (p.3):

> '...it does not help to act as an expert or teacher, nor to encourage parents to look to you for answers....Basically, parents need to be encouraged to see that they are different, that other people's answers may not work for them, that they have to find their *own* answers.'

The same guide goes on to suggest that the skills required to lead groups are very much the same as those being taught in the programme, principally encouragement and listening. Listening, in the sense of allowing each individual to be understood and to have their views respected, is emphasised above all. The author's advice is to:

'Trust the process; members who have a sense of being listened to can feel free to change and grow at their own pace.'

Edwards and Townsend (1993) in the programme Working with Parents for Change, define the group leader's role rather differently (p.13):

'As the group develops you should view yourself as a facilitator or enabler. Your role will be to help the group move along, contributing knowledge and other skills as necessary. You should avoid presenting yourself as having all the answers.'

Their Group Leader Handbook goes on to give helpful and practical advice about planning a group, setting the tone, guidelines on running a discussion, and dealing with problems in groups.

A somewhat more directive role is proposed for group leaders of the EPIC (Everyday Problems in Childhood) programme, which is a rather more structured series of 12 distinct topics:

'Your role as Group Organiser, once the group is under way, is to ensure that the materials are used as intended, and that the group does not digress too much from what it should be doing...You should always be prepared to be flexible and to use your own discretion. However, what you must avoid is a situation where the group is unable to complete a topic due to lack of time.'

Training and support for group leaders

Unlike the USA where parent education has developed into a separate educational profession, in the UK there is no such profession as *parent trainer* or *parent educator*. Facilitators come from a wide range of professions and backgrounds, and the parent education role is generally a secondary one. Their original professional training may have prepared them for a social worker, teacher, therapist or counsellor role, but perhaps on a one-to-one basis rather than with groups, and possibly with children rather than with adults. Alternatively, professional training may have put more emphasis on subject knowledge, for example health visitor, midwife, school nurse or nursery nurse training, rather than on the skills of teaching. The majority of parenting programmes described in this report have developed a training programme for leaders and facilitators. However, the extent and depth of the training varies considerably from, for example, a self-study Leader's Guide for the Family Caring Trust programmes, to a rigorous selection procedure and 140 hours of training spread over two or three terms for PIPPIN. Other examples are one week's training from Carolyn Webster-Stratton in California for the Parents and Children Series, and one day's training from Behaviour Management for the Coping with Kids programme. Several programmes adopt the apprenticeship model, whereby a newly trained facilitator works alongside an experienced one before leading a course herself or himself. A few programmes (for example, EPIC and What Can a Parent Do? (Family Caring Trust)) suggest that it is helpful for a new leader to have been a participant on a previous course. Table 7 lists the type of training for group leaders provided by the programmes included in this review.

Table 7:   Group leader/facilitator training

Name of programme	Type of training
ABC of Behaviour	6 x 1.5 hour sessions
Asperger Syndrome	Professional qualification + experience
Black Families Talking	Groupwork course
Coping with Kids (AD)	1 day by Behaviour Management
Coping with Kids (Kidderminster)	Professional knowledge + groupwork skills
Day Group Programme	Professional training (EP)
Effective Parenting (Cheshire)	Professional training (EP)
Effective Parenting (Herts)	8-session course (16 hours)
EPIC	Written notes for group leaders
Family Caring Trust	None, or apprenticeship model
Family Nurturing Network	16-hour foundation training Apprenticeship
Goal Planning Course	Professional training (EP)
Handling Children's Behaviour	4 x 2 hour sessions. Apprentice & cascade.
Help! I'm a parent	Written advice on leading groups
Living with Teenagers	Apprenticeship model (EP)
Mellow Parenting	Initial and on-going training
Newpin	Newpin provides in-service & induction
Open University	Associated group leader training. Cascade.
Parent Effectiveness Training	60-hour programme

continued ...

Table 7 (continued)

Name of programme	Type of training
Parenthood Group (YOI)	No specific training
Parenting course (Stockport)	Professional (EP & teacher)
Parent Network	150 hours over 6 months. In-service.
Parent Workshops (Southwark)	Professional (EP)
Parents against crime	1-day seminars/2-day training
Parent & Children Series	Must complete 2 groups with recognised trainer
Parents 'n' Kids	Groupwork/counselling
Parentwise	Professional training + commitment to method
Parentwise (Birmingham)	Non-specific
PIPPIN	200 hours over 3 terms
Positive Parenting (Durham)	Training for Trainers course
Positive Parenting (Leicester)	Lecturer trains HVs & SWs
Positive Parenting Packs	Outline courses being developed
Promoting Positive Parenting	Training for staff to run groups
Seven supertactics for superparents	None
Special Parenting Programme	Training from Head of Service
STEP	Associated training programme
Toddler Taming & Behaviour Management	Professional training & FE certificate
Working with Parents for Change	9 x half-days. Plans to cascade.

Glossary: EP Educational psychology   HV Health visitor   SW Social worker

A number of issues arise in relation to the training of facilitators. First, is it necessary at all? Programmes such as those published and marketed by the Family Caring Trust suggest not. Certainly having a 'trained' leader introduces the possibility of leaders having power and control over participants, rather than facilitator and participant being seen as equals. Assuming, though, that some element of training to lead parenting programmes is necessary:

- Who are the people who should be trained to undertake this work, and how should they be selected?
- Do they need to be parents themselves, for example?
- Should they be of the same cultural group as most of the participants?
- If potential facilitators are selected, are there then barriers to entry?
- How accessible are training programmes?
- What are the minimum standards of competence which facilitators should have, or should achieve during training?
- What are the core elements of a facilitator training course?
- How can facilitators best be supported in what can often be quite challenging and difficult work?
- How can standards be maintained? Particularly if the 'cascade' method of training is adopted – does the message become diluted or changed?
- How can recognition be given to those facilitators who undertake significant training to lead parenting skills groups?
- Should the limitations of the training be made explicit? For example, facilitators should not be expected to be able to solve all problems, to be counsellors or therapists.

A model of training

The following description of PIPPIN's selection, training and support programme offers one model. The staff of this organisation have done a considerable amount of thinking about the issues involved, and are continuously modifying the training programme in the light of experience. This description is presented here as a case study of one particular approach – there is no suggestion that this model would be suitable for all parenting programmes. It does, however, illustrate a particular response to some of the issues which people in this field are currently raising as concerns.

PIPPIN has developed a facilitator training programme which is externally accredited by the Open College Network. The training programme leads to PIPPIN's Certificate & Diploma in Facilitation and Groupwork Skills for Supporting the Parent-Infant Relationship. It is suitable for individuals who wish to become fully authorised PIPPIN facilitators, as well as for those who want to enhance their ongoing work in support for expectant and new parents. An ongoing feature of

PIPPIN's training philosophy is the use of self-assessment and assessment by peers. PIPPIN's facilitator training follows a number of steps:

Step 1 One-day introductory workshop.

Step 2 Completion and return of self-assessment and peer-assessment feedback form, together with a more detailed training application.

Step 3 Half-day selection workshop, during which graded experiential exercises allow applicants, peers and the PIPPIN training team to come to a consensus decision about the readiness of the individual to begin training. The key selection criteria are:

- previous experience with parents and infants;
- well-developed communication and problem-solving skills;
- sufficient awareness of own experiences with children, parenting and family life, without being overwhelmed by any past or current family relationship issues;
- ability and willingness to share and listen to personal experiences of the transition to parenthood, early parenting and family life in a supportive and non-judgmental manner;
- the ability to begin 'where each parent is.'

Step 4 Before entering a PIPPIN training programme all participants receive extensive course-related material, and Ethical Guidelines and Code of Practice, which they are asked to sign.

The training itself takes place on 21 days spread over three terms. During the first term participants learn effective facilitation and groupwork skills for working with women, men, couples and their children in the period of transition to parenthood. The second term offers a research-based theoretical and experiential exploration of the psychological dimensions of the transition to parenthood. Each participant undertakes a 20-hour infant observation module during the first two terms. In the third term, participants consolidate their training through personal reflection, reading and completing written assignments, leading up to a final review and assessment of the skill level achieved.

Participants can work towards PIPPIN's Certificate only, or for the combined Certificate and Diploma, at which point they can become fully authorised PIPPIN facilitators. Only then do they receive a Facilitator Manual and Parent Materials, which allows them to run the PIPPIN programme.

Step 5 During the post-training phase facilitators run their first few PIPPIN groups as Apprentice Facilitators, co-facilitating with an experienced facilitator, who provides ongoing support and training. While running PIPPIN groups all facilitators receive external supervision, in order to continue to evaluate their practice.

In a possible sixth step, after a suitable period of running PIPPIN groups, facilitators may eventually join the Trainer Development Programme, and eventually become PIPPIN trainers.

PIPPIN's facilitator training programme illustrates the establishment of a number of principles for such training. First, potential facilitators are, from the outset, made fully aware of the expectations of them, during selection, training and in leading groups. The objectives of the training are quite clear; the lines of support and supervision form an integral part of the overall programme – this is not an option for PIPPIN facilitators – they must agree to ongoing supervision. The issue of maintenance of standards is addressed by insisting on agreement to a code of ethics and a code of practice, which ensures that the PIPPIN programme is adhered to. The gradual assumption of responsibility for leading groups, and progress through the Trainer Development Programme provides another way of ensuring quality is maintained. The programme is externally validated, so that trainees have the option of acquiring competency-based qualifications which may be transferable to other related fields.

PIPPIN is a particularly specialised parenting education programme, which focuses on relationships during the transition to parenthood and is not typical of the majority of others referred to in this book. The associated specially developed training programme cannot, then, be seen as necessarily appropriate for others, or necessarily better than others but it does suggest ways to tackle some of the questions and issues in other settings.

A further example of a training programme is the series of eight weekly two-hour sessions provided for facilitators of the Effective Parenting (Hartley-Brewer and Hills) programme. Participants on this course, many of whom are teachers, are expected to develop the ability to communicate effectively in a group situation through the skills of active listening, appropriate responding and responsible assertive behaviour. The specific skills that are emphasised are attending, listening for meaning (content and feelings), the elimination of blocking responses and the increase of understanding empathetic responses and dealing with anger and criticism through the use of assertiveness skills. During the course a number of methods are used, such as demonstrations, discussion, simulations and drama.

The first seven sessions of the course cover:

- Introduction and facilitator's role;
- Working with the group;
- A sample session from the parenting programme;
- Preparing/planning for the series and the sessions;
- Use of media, materials and facilitator's manual;
- Dealing with sensitive or emotive issues;
- Key concepts and principles – the programme's common themes.

The eighth session is held after the course participants have started running the programme with parents, and provides an opportunity to assess and review their experience.

Participants in this course can choose to take up an accreditation option, which involves additional work, such as keeping a journal that will act as a personal learning record.

On-going support for group leaders

A number of people have highlighted the need for on-going support for group leaders and facilitators. The role can be difficult, and can result in considerable pressures on leaders. Several programmes recommend the involvement of co-leaders, or leader and assistant leader, so that discussion and de-briefing after sessions can be used to review the way in which the group has been handled. Participants may sometimes, in what they perceive as a safe and supportive environment, disclose very personal information about themselves or their relationships and, in addition to being able to handle such knowledge within the group, the facilitator may need to know how to help the person concerned, or where to direct him/her for further help. Strong emotions can sometimes be aroused in discussions around parenting, and leaders will need to be prepared to support individual participants when necessary, and ensure that other members of the group are also helped to cope with difficult situations.

There is widespread recognition of the need for on-going support for facilitators, and there are several examples of the way in which this is done. Parent-Link co-ordinators are frequently linked within a county or region, and can offer each other peer support and ongoing and updating training. In Anglican dioceses and other church networks where there is a programme of parent support, group leaders can be linked together for support. PIPPIN facilitators, as already noted, have a structured programme of supervision and support. A further need is for facilitators to continually review and update their skills.

This chapter has provided some insight into the range of organisations and individuals who offer and facilitate the programmes. The following two chapters now explore the programmes themselves in more detail – their theoretical base, value base, objectives and overall approach in Chapter 4, and their content, materials and methods in Chapter 5.

4. The programmes: overall approach and objectives

This chapter will consider, on the basis of the evidence generated by the survey, what we know about the overall approach adopted by the various group-based parenting programmes in use in the UK. Are there links between the specific objectives of the programme and the overall approach adopted? What are the different value bases and theoretical bases on which programmes operate? And how are all of these interrelated?

Overall approach

There are a number of ways of describing the overall approach of programmes, or the way in which they are presented. They can tend to empower parents, or alternatively to control them; they can start from where parents are, enriching and reinforcing the skills they already have, or alternatively, they can start with the problems or deficits; they can give advice and information in a didactic way – as coming from the 'experts' – or, alternatively, it can be offered in a more suggestive or advisory manner. In attempting an assessment about where parenting programmes were positioned in relation to these three different approaches, it was possible to draw on a range of sources of information questionnaires, reports, articles and the materials themselves. Where there was sufficient information (for 30 of the 38 programmes), it was then possible to make a judgement about which approach each programme tended to use. Almost half appeared to use an enrichment or reinforcement approach, rather than a deficit approach which started with the problems. Again, just over half the programmes used an advisory or suggestive approach, as opposed to just less than half which adopted a more didactic teaching approach. All 30 programmes tended to use an empowering approach, rather than a controlling strategy with parents.

At first sight, there would seem to be a contradiction between this last claim and the tendency of about half the programmes to present material in a didactic way, and also of about half to use a deficit rather than an enrichment model. Particular examples of didactic approaches came from among the group of programmes whose primary approach was 'behavioural', where techniques were taught. Professionals had perceived, or parents had themselves acknowledged, that they had problems in handling their children's behaviour. So that although the intention was to empower parents by offering them strategies to overcome their difficulties, the basis for the intervention was generally some apparent failure on the part of the parents. One example of such a programme is Coping with Kids, which tends to start with identification of difficulties, and whose methods aim to empower parents to deal with these difficulties. At the other end of the scale, Positive Parenting (Durham) begins with a positive recognition of parents' own strengths, and goes on to enrich these in an empowering way.

Earlier chapters have already pointed to the diversity of parenting programmes, especially in terms of their objectives, their content, and the methods they employ. It is the combination and interaction of these three elements, then, which can be said to result in the final form of any particular programme. A number of additional factors, though, can be seen to impinge on the way in which a programme is presented and is received by participants: the parents themselves – their needs, values and culture; the facilitators' own culture and values and perspective; and the changing state of knowledge, which is in turn influenced by research, legislation and policy. This complex picture can be represented diagrammatically as shown in Figure 2. The interactions represented here are multidirectional, resulting in a dynamic process largely in response to parent participants' needs and reactions to the material presented. This requires a particular sensitivity on the part of facilitators, in order to strike a balance between his or her own values and aims, and those of the participants. This interactive model provides some explanation for the fact that so many different programmes have been developed by different authors and presenters, each with their own ideas about aims and values which will best meet the needs of participants.

Figure 2: Factors influencing parenting programmes

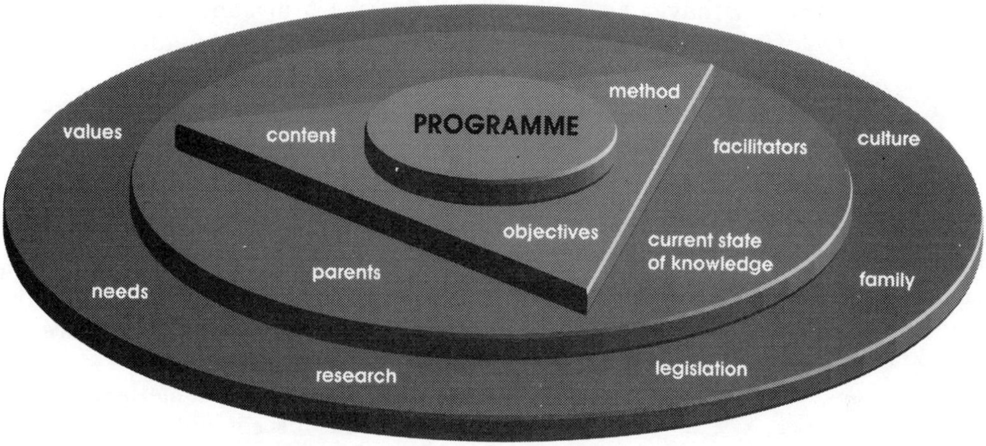

Value base

No parenting programme can be truly value-free. Both the orig-
inators of programmes and the facilitator of an individual
group come with their own value-laden 'baggage'. Some of these
values may come from professional training, others from
upbringing, from ethnicity and culture, and yet others from
changes in fashion regarding child rearing practices. By no
means all programmes state their value base explicitly, either
within the content of the materials, or as perceived by programme providers. Respondents representing 16 different programmes reported that the programme had a particular value
base (see Table 8). Respondents from a further 17 programmes
reported that their programme had no particular value base,
and five made no reply on this question.

Table 8:   Stated value base of programmes

Name of programme	Value base
ABC of Behaviour	Behaviour is learned and can change; parenting skills can be taught; strategies not always practised.
Coping with Kids (Kidderminster)	Parenting is not easy, there are no set methods. Parenting is the most important link with their child.
Effective Parenting	Confident parents will relate better to children and be better able to support growth and development.
Family Caring Trust	Developing responsibility and autonomy in children. Christian ethos.
Fun & Families	Parental choice in selecting behaviours to change and methods used. Also anti-discriminatory.
Handling Children's Behaviour	Broadly Christian ethos of self-worth to encourage happy/stable family life.
Help! I'm a parent	Christian.
Mellow Parenting	Capacity for parents to grow/develop at any age, and can make/remake relationships.
NEWPIN	Respect, support, equality, empathy.
PET	Person-centred principles.
Parent Network	All have the right to learn about ourselves, express ourselves and feel we matter and are heard.
PIPPIN	Parents and infants are individuals worthy of respect.
Positive Parenting (Miller)	Parents get better at parenting (a job) by being given appropriate ongoing support.
Positive Parenting (Sutton)	Happier children – happier parents.
Positive Parenting Packs	Judaeo/Christian underlying ethos.
Special Parenting Programme	Programme geared to level of learning of parents with learning disabilities.

It can be seen from Table 8 that four programmes reported that they were underpinned by Christian principles (Family Caring Trust, Handling Children's Behaviour, Help! I'm a Parent and Positive Parenting Packs). Only one of these – Help! I'm a Parent – appears to be explicit about this. The Family Caring Trust programmes all incorporate an optional Christian-based reflection for the end of each session, but suggest that this period is used for general reflection and relaxation by those who do not want a religious dimension. The statements of value made by the programmes vary considerably in the way they are expressed, both between programmes and also between different respondents on behalf of the same programme, but the majority have at their heart the concept that people – both adults and children – deserve to be valued in their own right.

The importance of programmes clearly stating, and operating by, their value base cannot be over-emphasised. Parents have a right to know, from the outset, whether the programme's values are likely to coincide with their own. A complete match may not be necessary, since sensitivity on the part of facilitators, and flexibility in the use of materials (in particular, the use of illustrations and case studies), and in the involvement by parents in setting their own goals, will help to minimise the differences. Wolfendale (1992) emphasises the importance of sensitivity in this context (p.30):

> 'In a multicultural, pluralistic society the challenge becomes one of juxtaposing the developmental 'universals' which most children acquire against the unique and highly particular circumstances in which all child-rearing takes place. Family practices in preparing and eating food, disciplining children and training them socially are undertaken within and are part of the family frame of reference, based on parents' own upbringing..., their societal/cultural inheritance and possibly their religious routines and customs. Sensitivity to individual family differences is paramount if we are to avoid charges of, at worst, *racist* responses...'

Allan (1994), in an article describing a study of parenting education programmes in Melbourne, Australia, also highlights the importance of 'parenting education programmes making clear their value base and the assumptions underlying the programmes.' Her concern is that some programmes lead to a perpetuation of dominant beliefs about gender roles. She says (p.357):

> 'There must be a move from gender neutral assumptions and language, and programmes need to provide opportunities for individ-

uals collectively to make links between their own experiences as mothers and fathers and the factors that have helped shape these experiences. Such principles will help foster a critical perspective that will keep in question dominant ideologies that can so disadvantage parents, particularly mothers.'

Chapter 7 pursues further this question of the importance of underpinning values in the context of standards and quality of programmes, and offers a self-evaluation exercise by which programme organisers may identify and demonstrate a range of underpinning values incorporated in the programme.

Theoretical base

Reference has already been made in Chapter 1 to the influence of early theorists and practitioners in the field of parenting education, and definitions of the various theoretical approaches provided. These influences have resulted in a diversity of approaches, some still clearly preserved as the main influences, such as in the PET and STEP programmes, both of which are widespread in the USA. This survey sought to discover which, if any, theoretical principles underpinned the various programmes in use in the UK. Respondents to the questionnaire were asked to say whether any of the following formed the theoretical base of the programme: humanistic; social learning/behavioural; psychoanalytic; family systems; any other background; or eclectic (incorporating a range of approaches). The results are displayed in Table 9.

Table 9:   The theoretical base of parenting programmes

Theoretical base	Number of respondents
Social learning/behavioural	39
Eclectic	17
Humanistic	16
Family systems	15
Other	12
Psychoanalytical	7

As Table 9 shows, one of the most striking features to emerge from this request was the large number of respondents (39 of the 51 returned questionnaires) who reported that the programme incorporated social learning/behavioural principles. Of these 39, 12 respondents indicated that this was the *only* theory on which they were based, with the remainder incorporating other influences as well. The other strong feature of the responses was the evidently eclectic nature of many of the programmes, drawing on a variety of different theories. Family Caring Trust, for example, reportedly incorporates humanistic, social learning/behavioural, and family systems theories with the emphasis falling on family systems and the influence of Adler and Rogers. Among others adopting an eclectic approach were Effective Parenting, PIPPIN and Parent Network. In the case of PIPPIN, this was described as an integrated approach, inferring that the various elements were integrated together, rather than simply added one to another.

Those programmes which stated additional theoretical foundations upon which their programmes were based named the following (some thus apparently tending to confuse value base with theoretical base):

- Christian
- Attachment theory
- Feminist, when looking at issues affecting mothers
- Person-centred (Rogerian)
- Mediated learning experience
- Educational – enhancing achievements by making parents more aware
- Developmental. Integration of developmental systems, via a humanistic approach
- Judaeo/Christian
- Developmental perspective
- Mainly family systems, Adlerian, Rogerian
- Strong problem-solving approach, start with positives
- Programme is not prescriptive, does not provide set answers.

Despite the replies of individual respondents, in most cases it proved quite difficult to find such acknowledgements in the materials themselves. Moreover, where there was more than one respondent for a single programme there were frequently discrepancies in their replies. It seems likely, then, that whereas the original author or developer of a programme was quite clear about the theories on which it was based, further down the line this was not always known to facilitators, or had become so diluted that it was not obvious.

Objectives

The aims and objectives of a parenting programme will be, to some extent at least, linked with its theoretical base and value base, and will play some part in determining its overall approach. A programme such as Handling Children's Behaviour, for example, which aims to help parents change their children's behaviour, is based solely on social learning/behavioural principles, whereas the Family Nurturing Network, whose aim is to change relationships within the family, is based largely on family systems theories. It was no surprise to find that in such a diverse group of programmes, respondents described their objectives in very different ways. Examples of all the following (often in combination rather than sole objectives) were found:

General objectives

- to change attitudes
- to improve parenting skills
- to improve coping skills
- to increase knowledge and understanding
- to improve parents' confidence and self-esteem
- to build family relationships
- to increase understanding
- to recognise parents' own needs
- to empower parents in their role
- to share views, ideas and information with other parents
- to raise children's self-esteem
- to improve the quality of life for parents and children
- to improve communication between parents and children
- to develop children's abilities
- to promote positive, nurturing parenting
- to give instruction in good parenthood and family relations
- to support and encourage parents.

More specific objectives

- to change parents' own behaviour
- to help parents change their children's behaviour
- to recognise and respect children's needs and be more child-centred
- to provide strategies for managing difficult behaviour
- to encourage an assertive style of parenting
- to help parents value and praise children

- to improve home-school links
- to reduce/prevent physical, emotional and verbal abuse of children
- to allow parents to recognise their own skills.

There are two things to note about this list of objectives. First, the wide range of different objectives in a group of programmes, all of which are perceived and described as 'parenting programmes'; and second, the very general nature of some of these objectives – especially those in the top half of the list.

Conclusion

Attempting to find any common denominators amongst these programmes in terms of links between overall approach, value base, theoretical base and objectives is a difficult task. The differences appear to be greater than the similarities, so that, for example, there are programmes whose objectives may be quite similar, but which use a different approach to achieve them. There are programmes which share similar value bases, but whose objectives are different. Perhaps the most useful conclusion to be drawn at this point is that amongst a wide range of people and organisations aiming to provide parenting education and support through a group-work method, there is an equally wide range of ideas about the best way to do this, and to meet the needs of a variety of parents.

5. The programmes: content, methods and materials

Having explored the theoretical ideas and the values on which these parenting programmes are based, and considered how these relate to the objectives and overall approach adopted by programmes, this chapter sets out to examine the contents, methods and materials in rather more detail. During the course of the review in 1994/95 a rich collection of course outlines, structures, topics, written materials, tapes, videos and handouts associated with these materials was assembled. These range from short topic booklets to quite extensive texts, some published, others just photocopied sheets. Brief descriptions are included in Appendix I and the full collection is housed in the library at the National Children's Bureau.

The content of any programme will, of course, derive quite closely from its objectives. Furthermore, the content of a programme cannot be entirely separated from the methods used in its implementation. However, for the purposes of this chapter, and to ensure clarity, these two aspects of parenting programmes are introduced separately. In the context of an educational process, though, the two are closely interconnected.

Content

Can this survey throw any light on the way in which programme content is selected? What are the principles which guide its selection? Can we show that content is, indeed, related to desired objectives? And can different content be used to achieve the same objectives? Or the same content to achieve different objectives? To what extent is the programme content offered as a complete package for participants to take or leave, or to what extent can parents influence content?

Harman and Brim (1980) suggest that there are two central foci regarding the content of parent education programmes:

first, imparting knowledge about child development; and, second, the provision of a range of advice and guidance on matters related to the parenting role. The present survey suggests the addition of one more category: that of a discussion of parenting itself, and parents' own needs. Broadly, the content of the majority of programmes included in this study can be divided into three main groups (seven subjects in total), These, together with the number of programmes which incorporates each of them, are as follows (Table 10):

Table 10:   Summary of contents of programmes

Main content of programmes	No. of programmes
• Advice and guidance on 5 main topics:	
– management of children's behaviour	26
– communication	17
– relationships and families	12
– problem solving	13
– handling stress	4
• Information about child development	13
• Parenting role and parents' own needs	9

Additionally, there were two programmes in which the content was not specified in detail since it is dependent on choice and definition by the parents attending on each and every occasion.

The way in which these seven content topics are combined in the different programmes is of some interest. Not surprisingly, the simpler the objective, the simpler the content. For example, there were seven 'behavioural' programmes whose content appeared to be limited to addressing only the issue of behaviour management. At the other end of the scale, the more complex and extended programmes, such as NEWPIN, PIPPIN and Parentwise, combined six different topics in their content. Few programmes appeared to offer an identical combination of topics, although there were close similarities between some as, for example, between the Family Caring Trust programme What Can a Parent Do? and the STEP programme.

Structured or flexible?

Analysis of the materials suggests that 36 of the 38 programmes included in this survey are presented in a structured, topic-based or theme-based way. The remaining two, as already noted, adopt a much looser structure in which the detailed content is agreed by each group of participants attending the programme. This high level of structure is, of course, unsurprising in the context of this survey which is concerned with the more formal, replicable type of programme. There is, indeed, a whole range of work outside of this, which is more loosely based and flexible, some of it fairly transient, such as that undertaken in family centres, parents' centres, home-school links projects, and many more. This area of work would merit a survey of its own, since no systematic information about it has been collected hitherto.

It would be incorrect, though, to leave the impression that the more formally structured programmes are entirely lacking in flexibility, or do not respond to parents' own needs, interests and wishes. Indeed, the very focus on group discussion and the group process allows parents to use illustrations and examples drawn directly from their own concerns, so that topics can become very personalised and relevant to individuals. Furthermore, several examples have emerged of group leaders adapting the programmes to suit particular groups' concerns: reducing the number of sessions, altering the order, selecting topics for a more workshop-type approach, and allowing individuals or the group to take time to thoroughly explore an issue or solve a problem. This raises again two issues referred to earlier – the skills of group leaders and facilitators, and the importance of the group process itself, regardless of the formal content in this type of approach to learning.

The survey questionnaire attempted to explore this flexibility in some detail, asking "Do parents' expressed needs and wishes influence the content of the programme?". The responses indicated a high degree of responsiveness to such needs and wishes of parents, and an adaptation or pacing of the programme according to parents' feedback and desire to include different topics. Typical responses to this question were:

'The content is flexible – there is a set structure, but can take into account specific needs arising in the group.'

'We would use a parent's own problem or experience if more relevant than an example in the book or on the tape.'

'The course has been changed after evaluation by fathers.'

'The modules are designed to flexibly adapt to parents' agendas.'

Themes or topics?

One other difference which emerged between the programmes surveyed was whether they were essentially *topic* based, or whether they were *theme* based. EPIC, for example, begins and ends with themes – such as *A positive approach to parenting, Dealing with Difficulties, Problem Solving* – but deals with topics, such as *Sleep Problems, Eating, Dressing* – through the central part of the programme. Both Parent Network and What Can a Parent Do? tend to concentrate on themes, such as listening, communicating and encouragement. Other programmes also follow this pattern, and relate the themes to specific topics as the programme progresses. This may be a more fruitful way for parents to learn skills and techniques which can be used in a variety of situations.

Other influences on programme content

Other influences on programme content were explored in the survey, participants being asked whether the content was influenced by dimensions such as class differences or socioeconomic differences of participants; cultural differences of participants; children's rights issues; and the need to address stereotypical roles of mothers and fathers. Some of these issues have already been referred to in Chapter 2, but it is worth reconsidering them specifically in relation to programme content.

Socioeconomic differences

The responses indicated a sensitivity on the part of programme leaders and authors to different intellectual and literacy levels, for example:

> 'Great efforts are made to make the programme accessible to all, irrespective of attainment.'

> 'We undertook wide testing and reading of material, especially checking that the case studies had variety.'

> 'Literacy levels determine the media used, and the amount of written advice/support available.'

There was, however, an acknowledgement by at least one programme that although it worked well over a wide socioeconomic range of participants, it was difficult for people with poor reading and writing skills. On the contrary, a respondent from one of the more widely used programmes suggested that:

> 'We encourage mixing of socioeconomic groups – they have bonds they did not suspect.'

Cultural differences

This question elicited a range of responses from programme providers and authors, from those which clearly attempted to recognise and incorporate the concept of 'difference' into the programme, to those which acknowledged some universal child-rearing themes which can be seen to transcend differences and be common to all parents. Thus:

'We openly acknowledge that parents may have different beliefs, and respect individual mores.'

'Facilitators are encouraged to collect examples which support principles of different cultures.'

'The basic feelings of love, hate, hurt, loneliness etc are common to all cultures and understood by all cultures.'

Children's rights

Almost all the responses heavily emphasised children's rights as being the cornerstone of their programme's belief system. For example:

'Children's rights are at the forefront of our minds, and accommodated in the workshops.'

'[Children's rights] are of paramount importance, individual respect for each child is taught from the very first hour.'

'Respect for children within a framework of adults exercising proper parental authority.'

This third quotation from the questionnaires reminds us that, despite the apparent overwhelming agreement about the importance of children's rights, there may be on occasions tensions that need addressing between parental rights and children's rights. More could perhaps be done by parenting programmes to tackle the notion of parental responsibility, which, within the UN Convention of the Rights of the Child, underpins the expression of children's rights.

Mother and father stereotypes

This question, like some others, elicited a wide range of responses:

'Very openly addressed. Parents given skills to negotiate roles and responsibilities.'

'The parenting role is emphasised, not the stereotypes.'

'[The programme] does not set out to adopt any stance on this issue.'

One programme which works mainly with quite disadvantaged groups of parents, mainly mothers, raised the sensitivity of this issue for some cultural groups, and also for some women who might not 'dare' to oppose their partners on this issue.

Many of the dimensions discussed in the preceding section are not only challenging in their own right, but there may also be a question about how realistic it is for all programmes to include them. The specific aims and objectives of programmes may be quite narrowly defined, and any attempt to incorporate all these broader aspects may risk compromising the main objectives. Chapter 6 revisits this issue, and suggests a way in which such values and principles can be said to *underpin* a programme's objectives, perhaps forming part of the process involved, without necessarily forming a specific part of the programme content.

Length of programmes

The period of time over which these content topics are presented varies widely. A few programmes may be single one-day or half-day workshop sessions, others can extend to as many as 15 or more. In some cases, such as NEWPIN for example, the group programme is only one part of a more complex programme which involves working with the whole family. In general, though, the majority of courses run over eight to ten weeks, each for a two-hour session. Some group leaders report that they reduce the length of the course where they feel that for some parents a long commitment is out of the question. Others decide to lengthen the programme in order to provide more flexibility to include topics of parents' own choosing.

Content and age of children

As noted earlier, the majority of programmes surveyed are intended for parents with young children. This is undoubtedly a reflection of the fact that this is an age where parents often find it hard to handle children's growing independence and feel that they need help. Another stage at which parents often feel particularly vulnerable is when their children become adolescents. In response to this some programme providers offer programmes specifically for parents of teenagers, generally as a follow-up to basic parenting programmes. Examples are:

- Parent-Link   Living with Teenagers
- Family Caring Trust   The Teen Parenting Programme
- Centre for Fun &
    Families   Living with Teenagers
- Surrey Educational
    Psychology Dept   Living with Teenagers
- STEP   Parenting Teens

The content of this group of programmes is similar for them all, covering such themes as behaviour and needs, conflict, negotiating solutions to conflict, power and authority.

Methods

Content and method are, of course, closely interrelated and in turn firmly linked to the primary objectives of the programme. Choice of method may also reflect a leader's background and experience. Group discussion forms a major part of all these programmes. It is here perhaps that the skills of the facilitator are most strongly tested, in ensuring the participation of all members of the group and not allowing one individual to be over-dominant. In some programmes, for example NEWPIN, it is the group process itself which is considered important in helping people to be aware of their own participation. Table 11 provides a picture of the frequency of different methods used in these 38 parenting programmes.

It is hardly surprising that group discussion should come top of the list, and used by all programmes, in a sample of programmes mainly defined by that criterion. The second most commonly used method, information giving, is recognised as a method as well as forming part of the content (see Table 10).

The first six methods listed in Table 11 were presented in a questionnaire as a predefined list, and respondents asked to tick all that they used. The remaining 10 come into the category of 'other' methods used by programmes, and are drawn from descriptions supplied by respondents. Some examples of the way in which these methods are used by the various programmes may be helpful at this point.

Table 11:   Frequency of use of different methods used in groups

Methods used in parenting programmes	No. of respondents
Group discussion	38
Information-giving	33
Audiotape/videotape	21
Role play or drama	20
Self-analysis/self-reflection	19
One-to-one discussion	16
Exercises/activities	11
Practice skills/homework	11
Reading	10
Share views, ideas, information	6
Parents and children work on same topics	4
Modelling behaviour	1
Mediated learning	1
Prayer	1
Record-keeping	1
Psychotherapy	1

Exercises and activities

Exercises and activities used in programmes vary widely in complexity. At one end of the scale, for example, an invitation to parents to list three items of behaviour in their children with which they are not happy (Positive Parenting). At the other end of the scale a quite complex listing and ranking exercise related to self-awareness and needs (Parent Network). The first is part of a six-module programme, described as promoting 'a method of behaviour management...which draws on a whole range of parenting skills.' The second was used in the 'Needs and Wants' session of a 12-topic course.

Skills practice/homework

The majority of the programmes encourage participants, either formally or informally, to practice the skills worked on in the session with their children at home. The expectation is then that a discussion of participants' success and progress will form part of the next session. Sometimes (Family Caring Trust programmes, for example), there is an expectation that participants will prepare for the following session by reading the relevant section of the handbook. In other programmes facilitators hand out at the end of the session articles or booklets which reinforce the topic covered that day. For some programmes, homework consists of record keeping of, for example, instances of certain behaviours in their children, or charts or grids to record changes in behaviour.

Reading

The amount and complexity of reading material in these programmes varies very considerably. The ABC of Behaviour, for example, is produced in large format, with large print and plenty of cartoon-type illustrations. Sentences are short, and statements clear. The STEP parents' handbook introduces more complex concepts, such as reflective listening, but still with plenty of examples and colourful illustrations. In Parent Network the listening topic runs over three booklets, and three sessions of the course. Some programmes, such as Positive Parenting, restrict the amount of reading parents need to do, but suggests other sources for those who do want to do more.

Share views, ideas, information

It goes without saying that one of the strengths of the groupwork method is the opportunity for participants to share their ideas and views with each other. As mentioned in Chapter 3, an important role of the facilitator is to ensure that each group member has the opportunity to play an equal part in this sharing. Parents attending group parenting programmes often comment that the biggest thing they get out of the experience is listening to other people's views and experiences, without feeling that they always have to adopt other people's solution to the problem.

Parents and children work on the same topics

Very few of the programmes surveyed for this book work with parents *and* children, either together or separately. One notable exception is the Family Nurturing Network, in which the same topic is addressed at an appropriate level by both parents and children, and the session usually ends with a short joint session to cement the lessons learned. Mellow Parenting involves video work with parents and children. NEWPIN includes a Family Play Programme, with parents and children, as well as separate programmes for adults. The programmes run by Exploring Parenthood, Parents Against Crime and Parents 'n' Kids, both run parallel children's or young people's sessions.

Modelling behaviour

Only one respondent offered this method of work as one used in her programme. However, it would seem likely that for all these programmes, the role of the group leader or facilitator is extremely important in this respect. The group process itself is also sometimes used to model or reflect what may be happening in the family group.

Mediated learning

This method has been identified in only one programme, the Parentwise project in Plymouth, although it may well be present in a less overt form in a number of other programmes. The method is based on the belief that a person's cognitive potential and development are structured by the ways in which experienced and competent adults mediate that individual's learning experiences. This can be either directly or through community processes (for example, select, share, interpret, develop, invest meaning into those experiences). This mediation is an overt process, recognised and explained by the mediator to the learner. This project believes that this has implications, not just for understanding interactions between parents and their children, but between project workers and the parents. So, for example, as the programme co-ordinator explains (Jones, 1994) session leaders may describe to parents their intentions as:

'To help you to actively enjoy your baby and to enjoy being a parent.'

and their own values:

'As some of the professionals working with lots of children we believe it is important that we share our knowledge and experience with you.'

and their hopes for generalisation:

'By being able to use these ways of thinking about what questions to ask, and who to ask, we hope you will ask questions, not just in these sessions, but when you take your child to the clinic, the doctor's surgery, to school, or anywhere else for advice or help.'

Jones continues his explanation of mediated learning:

'Simply speaking, this can be understood as a highly structured way of being "upfront" with people, and conveying clearly how one sees one's role in the parent education process. Parentwise believes that careful analysis of the ways in which we can be "upfront" can help to engage in the process of learning those parents who might otherwise feel challenged, suspicious, devalued or alienated. Mediation of learning is felt to be a promising way of understanding the interactional processes in parent education. Session leaders value the learning experiences of parents in interaction with their children as unique, and respect the fact that they may be following unique developmental paths. Parents are encouraged to make sense of the ways in which socioeconomic, community, cultural or political factors are constraining or facilitating the developmental process of becoming a parent. They are also encouraged to articulate and share that understanding. Session leaders and parents are then in a learning interaction where roles, values and intentions are "upfront", but where differences can be acknowledged. Session leaders have a clear agenda directed towards ways of achieving parenting in the community which can best realise children's potential for growth and development in all areas.'

A fairly full description of this method of mediated learning has been provided, partly because it may not be widely known or understood by all readers, and secondly, because it would seem to be a model which could usefully be used with other groups of people who, faced with other methods, may, as Jones suggests, feel 'challenged, suspicious, devalued or alienated.'

Prayer

The programmes produced by the Family Caring Trust provide for a period of reflection during each session, which can be used for prayer and spiritual contemplation if wished, or simply for a period of quiet reflection on the session. One other Christian-based programme, Help! I'm a parent, also includes elements of prayer and meditation.

Record keeping

Only one programme reported that record-keeping was used as a method. However, there is evidence from a number of others that participants are, indeed, asked to undertake various recording activities – lists, charts, diagrams, and so on. This method allows parents to focus particularly on personal family situations, to be aware of change taking place, and to continue their involvement with the programme between sessions.

Rewards

A number of programmes, especially those focusing on behaviour change in children, promote the use of rewards – in recognition of wanted behaviour, as evidence of praise for family members, and as a way of raising children's self-esteem. The rewards might take a number of forms – treats, extra privileges, 'certificates', or stickers to be added to charts. One programme, Coping with Kids, also sometimes uses rewards for parents attending the programme. Raffle tickets are handed out to parents who come to each session, and also during sessions to parents who contribute to the discussion, do the exercise, share an experience with the group, and so on. At the end of the session the raffle is drawn, and the lucky winners depart with a prize, and may well be more likely to come to the following week's session!

Materials

The materials used for these programmes are described in summary in Appendix I. Materials are published by 23 programmes. The remaining 15 programmes have either developed their own materials, using their own resources, or make use of published books and other material. Within the 'published' group, there are two principal models: a leader's manual, which usually includes handouts for parents which can be copied as needed; and a parent's handbook, usually together with leader's handbook or materials. These are listed in Table 12.

Table 12:   Published materials

Organisation / programme	Publications
ABC of Behaviour	Parents' book – *The ABC of Behaviour*
	Parents' book - *Assertive Discipline for Parents*
Coping with Kids	Parents' book – *Parent Resource Guide*
	Leaders' guide
Effective Parenting	Manual – *Facilitator's Manual*
EPIC	Topic leaflets & organiser's notes + tape
Family Caring Trust	Book & leader's guide for each programme, + tape
Family Nuturing Network	Handbooks & leader's manuals
Handling Children's Behaviour	Leader's book
Help! I'm a parent	Kit – video cassettes, course sheets, book
NEWPIN	Co-ordinator's material
Open Univeristy	Book for each module
PET	Textbook, workbook and instructor manual
Parent-Link	Handbooks for each theme/session
Parents against Crime	Course leader's guide
Parents & Children Series	Video vignettes
Parents 'n' Kids	Manual
PIPPIN	Leader's manual and parents' notes
Positive Parenting (Miller)	Handbook in ringbinder file
Positive Parenting (Sutton)	8 booklets *Managing Difficult Young Children*
Positive Parenting Packs	Packs and booklets, leaflets
Promoting Positive Parenting	Range of bookets, video and audiotapes, packs for group leaders
Seven Supertactics	Parents' booklet
STEP	Parents' Handbook and other programmes
Working With Parents for Change	Pack with handbook and 4 topic books + handouts

By way of illustration, the following pages contain a more detailed description of six sets of materials: three for programmes categorised as 'behavioural', and three for programmes classified as 'relationships' programmes.

Working with Parents for Change: A parent group-work approach to managing behaviour (Edwards, P and Townsend, L 1993)

This material is in the form of a wallet containing five 24-page A4 size booklets, each with a glossy, colour cover illustrated with children's drawings. The five titles are:

1. Group Leader Handbook
2. Parenting
3. Handling difficult behaviour
4. Families
5. Developmental issues

The Group Leader Handbook contains guidelines for using the package, suggesting that it should be regarded as a framework of information and ideas, and should be used flexibly as appropriate for each group, with time given to the inclusion of ideas and material suggested by group members. The final part is given over to practical guidance on leading a group, covering the planning and setting up of the group, setting the tone and a discussion of the group leader's role.

The contents of each of the four following booklets comprises both information and guidelines for the group leader, and information sheets and activity sheets which can be copied for participants. An example, taken from the third booklet, is entitled *Why does he do it?* The Group Leader's section describes the purpose of the exercise and suggests a way of starting discussion. The corresponding parents' section is an exercise in which parents are asked to look at examples of behaviour and think in each case, why the child might do it, and what the parent should do about it, and why.

The exact way in which these materials are organised into a course, or series of sessions, is left very much to the group leader, the only definite advice being that the sections on *Parenting* and *Handling Difficult Behaviour* are used first, and in that order.

Figure 3:   Working with Parents for Change

Working with Parents for Change	Section 4

FAMILIES

Activity 1

**He knows
I love him!**

In the heat of the moment we often say things to our children which we may regret later.

What kind of messages about themselves and about your feelings towards them does your child receive from you?

A   Write down your three positive remarks you most often say to your child.

Example: *What a good boy*

Write down three negative remarks you most often say to your child.

Example: *Don't be so stupid.*

B   Do you think you should change some of the things you say to your child?

If so, what would you like to change?

From: Edwards, P and Townsend L (1993) *Working with Parents for Change*, vol 4, p 8. Strathclyde Regional Council. Reproduced with permission.

Positive Parenting (Miller, S, 1994)

These materials are published in the form of 35 A4-size looseleaf sheets in a ring binder file. After a short introduction explaining the aims of the materials, there follow six modules:

1. Using our existing strengths
2. Obstacles to change
3. Feeling good about ourselves
4. Planning for change
5. Parents: the flexible friends
6. Working together

The materials are written in an inclusive, first person, style: for example, 'We need to describe...' and 'We need clear evidence...' and '...several routines in our day...'. The modules are clearly laid out, with distinctive logos to identify where an activity requires writing, or discussion, or thinking. Key points are also regularly summarised. The modules can be used as stand-alone workshops, or arranged as a series of sessions. Throughout the modules there is an emphasis on goal setting exercises.

Figure 4:   Positive Parenting

26

Positive Parenting

The psychology of self esteem

The need to value ourselves is a first step to valuing others and developing self esteem.

When we say things like—

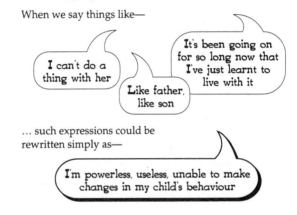

... such expressions could be rewritten simply as—

These feelings are all the more likely to erode our self esteem as parents, because they relate to very young—and therefore apparently—more manageable children.

There is a sense in which we may feel guilty because we 'ought' to be able to make things different.

Our apparent lack of influence over our children is so often patently obvious to family members and friends who may not always be sympathetic to our situation.

The care of young children is still largely unpaid, predominantly done by women, outside of any management or supervisory structure, and unnegotiated.

In a society which seems to measure a job's importance by the amount someone doing it earns, it is not surprising that those of us who are working with young children may feel undervalued at times.

From: Miller, S (1994) *Positive Parenting*. p.26. Newcastle-upon-Tyne, Formword Ltd. Reproduced with permission.

Handling Children's Behaviour

This programme of 10 sessions is set out in a 60-page A4-size bound book:

1. Types of behaviour
   - behaviour we complain about
2. Points to ponder
3. Rules
   - punishment/Consequences
4. Reinforcing behaviour
   - rules, consequences and consistency
5. Reinforcement/Reward
6. Play session
7. Recording
8. Relaxation
9. Review course
   - case studies
10. Evaluation of course

The pattern for each session is similar, and includes a review of previous sessions, a review of the previous week's homework, the current topic (usually involving exercises and discussion), this week's homework, and handouts. Most sessions include exercise or activity sheets which can be copied for parents.

The material is laid out in a somewhat less user-friendly way than either of the previous two programmes, and requires considerable familiarity with the material and preparation of each session by the group leader. It is explicitly arranged, however, and the required 'props' for each session clearly listed.

Figure 5:   Handling Children's Behaviour

Steps to be taken in 'calm down time'

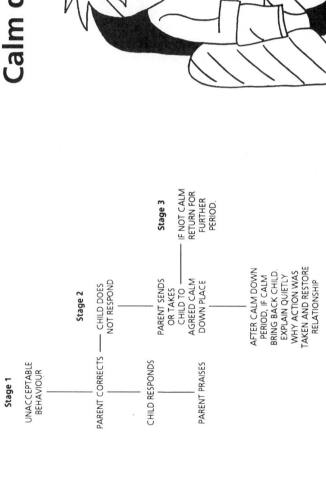

Calm down time

Stage 1

UNACCEPTABLE
BEHAVIOUR

Stage 2

PARENT CORRECTS —— CHILD DOES
                    NOT RESPOND

CHILD RESPONDS

PARENT PRAISES

PARENT SENDS
OR TAKES
CHILD TO
AGREED CALM
DOWN PLACE

Stage 3

IF NOT CALM
RETURN FOR
FURTHER
PERIOD.

AFTER CALM DOWN
PERIOD, IF CALM
BRING BACK CHILD.
EXPLAIN QUIETLY
WHY ACTION WAS
TAKEN AND RESTORE
RELATIONSHIP

From: Finch, G (1994) *Handling Children's Behaviour*, p.27. NCH Action for Children. Reproduced with permission.

What Can a Parent Do? (Family Caring Trust)

This programme is subtitled 'Simple practical skills to help parents be more responsible and effective'.

The materials comprise a Leader's Guide and a parents' handbook, which each participant is encouraged to buy for themselves. Both are published as bound books.

The sessions are intended to be run as an eight-session course:

1. What is your child looking for?
2. Becoming a responsible parent
3. Encouragement
4. Listening
5. Communicating about problems
6. Disciplining children
7. Talking things out together
8. Bringing it all together

The suggested sequence for each session is similar, consisting of:

- A brief introduction
- How everyone got on since the last meeting
- This week's topic (including exercise – Getting in Touch)
- Case studies from the cassette
- Improving your skills – skill practice
- Planning to apply the ideas in the week ahead
- Reflection (optional)
- Summing up
- Final details
- Socialising

At the end of each chapter a table sums up the main points of the session. 'Tips for Parents' and 'Comments from other Parents' close each chapter.

The Leader's Guide is detailed – setting out a complete script which can be followed through the session if wished, together with the transcript of the audio or video tape case studies.

The parents' handbook is illustrated with cartoons, and is clearly set out. The regular pattern, both in the way the sessions are run, and the way in which the handbook is set out, are helpful for what is a quite complex course with multiple objectives.

Figure 6:   What Can a Parent Do?

**GETTING
IN
TOUCH**

How often do you make these (or similar) remarks. Put a tick for each statement in the appropriate column.

	Never	Sometimes	Often

DISCOURAGEMENT
Why can't you be like ...
Nag, nag, nag ...
You're a cheeky brat!
Just look at your room, you filthy ...
Don't ... Don't... Don't
You're a very naughty (bold) girl!

PRAISE
What a beautiful picture!
You're terrific!
You look so wonderful!
You're such a good boy!

ENCOURAGEMENT
Thank you. That helps me.
So that's how you do it!
Congratulations. You've improved.
Will you help me with...

**PLANS
FOR NEXT
WEEK**

Who is your most discouraged child? In what ways can you encourage that child during the next week? Possibilities include: Being on the lookout for efforts and improvements and 'noticing' them ; trusting them with more responsibilities; saying 'thanks', 'please', 'sorry' and generally showing respect; spending more time with them, especially time listening to them; being cheerful and good-humoured yourself; being interested in them and in their world... You may like to write down your plans.

Plans... _____

Parent-Link

The materials for parents for this 12-session course are presented in a series of 16-page A5-format booklets:

Being a parent
Feelings
Sharing my feelings
Being a helper
Challenging
Being firm and gentle
Labels
Whose problem is it?
Introduction to listening
Reflective listening
Needs and wants

In addition, there is a handbook for parent support groups who decide to continue meeting after the formal course has finished.

These booklets are normally handed to participants at the end of each session, and the detailed plans for the sessions are available only to trained Parent-Link Co-ordinators. During sessions the materials are extended by the use of handouts and exercises.

NATIONAL CHILDRENS
BUREAU ENTERPRISES LTD
8 WAKLEY ST.
LONDON
EC1V 7QE
VAT REG. 645 1833 36

8/12/97

Developing Parenting
Prog.

8.50

~~Cheque~~
~~Cash~~

Figure 7: Parent-Link

Unhelpful responses

With the best will in the world we may set out to help people with a problem and either have no effect or make it worse. Common unhelpful responses include reassuring, taking their minds off it, denying the feelings, sharing our own problems to divert them from theirs, or simply giving "good advice".

criticising   *labelling*

diagnosing   *praising*

4

From: *Parent-Link: Reflective listening II*, p.3. Parent Network. Reproduced with permission.

Family Nurturing Network

There are three component parts to the Nurturing Programme used by the Family Nurturing Network in Oxford: The Parent Handbook, the Activities Manual for Parents, and the audiovisual programmes. The corresponding Nurturing Programmme for children is normally run alongside the parents' programme. The Parent Handbook contains short sections on the following themes and topics:

- Helping children learn appropriate behaviours
- Family rules and guidelines
- Establishing family rules
- Rewarding children's behaviour
- Praising yourself and your children
- Personal power
- Punishing children's behaviour
- Time out
- Why parents hit their children
- Our self-esteem and self-concept
- Needs and payoffs
- Behaviour payoffs
- Ages and stages: development of children
- Helping children manage their own behaviour
- Stress management techniques
- Communicating thoughts and feelings: I statements and you messages
- Nurturing ways to handle your anger
- Confrontation and criticism
- Rules for fair fighting
- Facts about AIDS
- Touch and talk
- Ignoring as behaviour encouragement
- Feelings! Nothing more than feelings
- Misery-making beliefs and better choices
- Problem-solving and decision making
- Negotiation and compromise

Figure 8:   Family Nurturing Network

Promoting Self-Praise in Children

Self-praise is a way children can learn the habit of praising themselves and boosting up their self-image. To help a child learn self-praise, parents need to describe how good the act must have made the child feel. Imagine yourself in the child's shoes, and describe the feeling. By promoting self-praise, children learn to be their own best friend and develop self-confidence.

"Tracie, I bet you feel good after cleaning your room."

To encourage children to use self-praise, parents should model the behavior for them. Praise yourself in the presence of your children whenever you do something well, or whenever you feel good about yourself. Modeling self-praise is an effective teaching procedure because children learn best by imitation.

How to Praise

To praise appropriately, follow the steps listed below:

1. **Focus your attention on the child and the situation—praise deserves your undivided attention.**

2. **Move close to the child—praise feels good by someone close to you.**

3. **Make eye contact with the child on the child's level. For instance, stoop down to make eye-contact with a five-year old—this makes it all the more special.**

4. **Gently touch the child—touch is a positive form of communication.**

5. **Look pleasant—everyone likes to see a happy face.**

6. **Praise your child for being or for doing.**

7. **Offer a hug to "seal" the nice words.**

Praise anytime — there is no such thing as too much praise!

From: Bavolek, S and Comstock, C (1991) *Nurturing Programme for parents and children 4 to 12 years*, Parent Handbook, p.15. Utah: Family Development Resources Inc. Reproduced with permission of the Family Nurturing Network, Oxford.

Conclusions

It might be assumed that one, perhaps rather obvious, conclusion could be drawn from this look at the content, methods and materials used by the parenting programmes surveyed: the more complex the objectives, the more complex the content and the materials used, and vice versa. But is this really true? A simple objective, for example, might be said to be one which is aiming to change children's behaviour. This apparently simple goal, however, disguises the fact that in the process a number of quite complex concepts may need to be discussed, information imparted, a range of skills learned and practised, self-esteem raised, and parents feel empowered to take some control. This is not to deny the fact that a programme which aims to take a broader look at the overall skills of parenting will not use a more extensive and in-depth approach, simply to suggest that an apparently simple goal, such as behaviour change, may involve the use of a surprisingly wide range of methods and content, organised in a variety of ways, and using a diversity of materials.

Having given some attention in the previous chapters describing and analysing these programmes, the next chapter examines what we know about their effectiveness.

6. Do parenting programmes work?

Family support initiatives of all kinds, including the parenting programmes which are the subject of this book, are receiving widespread attention at present. Their potential social benefits – for preventing child abuse, keeping families together, reducing crime, improving school-readiness, and so on, are widely debated and discussed. Many people involved in this area of parent education are convinced of its benefits, not least the parent participants who, almost universally report positively on the benefits of parenting programmes for themselves and their families. Others, such as funders and policy-makers, though, require better evidence than this in order to be convinced about the need to commit resources and shift policy in the direction of this preventative type of work. Moreover, quite apart from these 'macro' questions about effectiveness, it is of course morally and ethically necessary for programme providers to be sure that work of this kind with families is really what they want, and will enable parents to grow in self-confidence and take control of their lives.

This chapter, then, will explore some of the issues around evaluation and describe and comment on what we know already about the effectiveness of parenting programmes. In Chapter 7 we also offer a suggested framework for evaluation of parenting programmes.

What do we mean by 'effectiveness'?

The demonstration of effectiveness may take a number of different forms. At its most basic, this can be expressed by asking the question 'Does the programme achieve what it sets out to achieve?' Beyond that there may be a whole range of unknowns which require answers:

- Does attending a parenting programme have a positive effect on the way in which parents bring up their children?
- If there is a measurable effect, is it evident immediately, and how long does it last?
- Is there a positive outcome for children?
- Does their behaviour change?
- If change is detected, in parent or child, how can we be sure that attendance at the parenting programme is responsible for that change?
- If change is proven, what are the processes involved in allowing that change to come about?
- Does the programme meet the needs of participants?
- If an evaluation shows change, to what extent can that effect be generalised to replications of the programme, or to other programmes?
- Is one type of programme more appropriate for some parents than for others?
- And, importantly, are there any negative effects of attendance at a parenting programme?

Furthermore, an important factor in any evaluation in the social field is to first ask 'From whose perspective are we looking?' The various stakeholders in parenting programmes may have quite different perspectives: for example, there may be different views of effectiveness from parents, group leaders, organisers, funders and referring agencies.

Why evaluate?

Of course, there are many reasons why it is important to evaluate a project's work. All project staff need to know what is happening as a result of their work so that they can improve their practice, check their progress, perhaps act as a training resource and tell others about their work. A useful guide to evaluation (van der Eyken, 1992) suggests that there are a number of questions which may require answers:

- How successful is the project in achieving its original aims?
- How is the programme meeting the needs of parents and families?
- What has worked well, and what has not worked so well?

In addition to these questions about the project itself, it is important for programmes to know something about the impact of the programme on the lives of families. If there have been changes, by what processes have they been brought about?

There are likely to be several different audiences for the results of an evaluation, but the most important is the organisation or project itself. Evaluation is likely to throw up new questions, challenge assumptions, prompt ideas and so on, as well as providing a good basis on which to communicate with others doing the same sort of work, with funders and politicians.

What do we know already?

Evidence of the sort which is based on rigorous evaluation methods, about the effectiveness of parenting programmes in the UK is in short supply. There are a few sources, however, to which we can refer. Studies have been carried out in the USA, and also in Australia, over a period of years, and there is some evidence from these sources. Also, the present survey located 15 evaluation reports, of varying depth and rigour, and we shall report on what we know from these studies. First we will look briefly at some of the American and Australian evidence.

Dembo and others (1985) reviewed 48 evaluation studies of three different types of parenting education programmes in the USA: behavioural approaches, Parent Effectiveness Training (PET) and Adlerian approaches (as used in the STEP programme). Overall, these evaluations indicated that certain changes in parental attitudes and/or child behaviour were evident as a result of different educational approaches. However, the quality and type of research procedures varied greatly among the studies, and these reported changes were not always consistent and often depended on the type of assessment and educational approach used. The reviewers' critique of the methodology used in these 48 studies found that few studies approached all or most of the necessary criteria for a well-designed investigation. The research problems identified in many of the studies included lack of randomisation of subjects, absence or inappropriate use of control groups, failure to collect process data, and lack of long-term follow-up designs. Measurement problems included over-reliance on parents' self-reporting, the use of inappropriate measures, and measurement of general child-rearing attitudes rather than focusing on specific attitudinal change of parents towards their own children. Overall, these authors concluded that there were 'not enough well-

designed studies to draw definitive conclusions and implications about the general effectiveness of parent education, or
whether one type of program is more beneficial for a certain
type of family or person.'

Another more recent overall analysis of 24 parenting
programmes in the USA (Medway, 1989) concluded that these
programmes were effective in that both parents and children
showed improvements on a range of measures. However, like
Dembo, this author was critical of the studies themselves,
thus calling into question their findings.

Davies (1978) compared six parenting packages in use in
Australia, and suggested that each package tended to be
limited by its failure to accept values from other frames of
reference. In fact, she proposed that the more that different
theoretical elements can be blended into an eclectic approach,
the more scope there is for making programmes more relevant
to particular situations – age of child, particular behaviour
problems, particular home environment, and so on.

Notwithstanding the more positive outcomes for parents
and children already mentioned, Doherty and Ryder (1980)
raised a number of criticisms and caveats in relation to the
PET programme used widely in the USA. Their study went so
far as to suggest that PET introduced a number of possible
unwanted effects for individuals and families. The authors
suggest, and go on to explain at some length, that the programme tends to 'technologise' parent-child relationships;
that is makes harsh and unwarranted judgments about
parents; that it presents a simplistic formula for handling all
parent-child problems and that the programme is based on
questionable assumptions about family dynamics. A more
recent study of parenting education in Australia (Allan, 1994),
using the STEP (Systematic Training for Effective Parenting)
programme as a case study, argues that such programmes can
perpetuate dominant ideologies which can disadvantage
parents, especially mothers. She perceived little attempt to
differentiate between the roles of mothers and fathers, and no
encouragement to participants to question the status quo.

In summary, then, there appear to be three separate
messages coming from this reported research. Firstly, the
criticisms of the studies themselves, on methodological
grounds; secondly, the inability of many of these evaluation studies to demonstrate conclusively positive effects for

parents attending parenting programmes; and thirdly, the suggestion that some programmes may introduce possible negative impacts for some participants. Overall, this is not to suggest that parenting programmes *are* necessarily ineffective, rather that their effectiveness has been exceedingly difficult to demonstrate.

What has our own study told us?

The survey of parenting programmes provided two sets of information which contribute to this section: first, programme organisers' responses to the survey questionnaire; and second, written research reports which were available to us.

Effects reported by questionnaire respondents

The majority of respondents to the questionnaire (39 of the 51 respondents) reported that they had a monitoring or evaluation system in place to help them judge the success or otherwise of their programme. Only seven reported that they did not have either system in place, and five did not reply. For the majority of programmes, the monitoring system included, as a minimum, a record of attendance and a questionnaire or evaluation form through which parents could feed back their own views of the programme. For some, the record keeping was considerably more detailed, as for example, the Family Nurturing Network programme which included a weekly self-evaluation by parents, a family log and an end of course evaluation. Some of the self-completion evaluation forms tended to be limited to the opportunity for parents to express a view on how 'useful' or 'enjoyable' the course had been. Others gave opportunities to express views about different sessions, different approaches and whether their own or their children's behaviour or family relationships more generally had improved. These provided a more detailed and specific measure of effectiveness, albeit subjectively from the participants' point of view.

Self-reports by parents are generally enthusiastic, with many emphasising that they *feel* much more confident in their parenting, that they have acquired skills and knowledge that they did not have before, and that they have enjoyed the support of other parents with similar problems. This in itself must be seen as important feedback – parents are unlikely to learn or benefit from programmes unless they find the content and approach acceptable.

Lasting the course, and being motivated to do so, was seen as one indication that the programme must be meeting some of the parents' needs, although little attention appeared to have been paid to exploring the reasons why some participants dropped out. The survey asked about other criteria used to measure effectiveness. These varied according to the aims and objectives of the different programmes. For example, those programmes which set out to help parents bring about changes in their children's behaviour tended to use such perceived changes as a positive outcome. Others mentioned perceived changes in parents' own behaviour and their handling of their children, in order to bring about changes in children's behaviour. Programmes aimed more at improving family relationships overall tended to mention criteria such as whether the skills learned had been integrated into the family and their benefits felt more widely, and whether family relationships generally had improved. Only two responses actually mentioned a change in attitudes as being significant, although this may have been implied in others who talked about parents' feelings and enjoyment of their children. Five respondents mentioned a perceived increase in self-esteem and self-confidence as being significant for judgement of the effectiveness of a programme.

Respondents to this survey were asked about what changes had been noticed by group leaders, for both parents and children, as a result of attending a course. Some of the changes mentioned will probably have been taken from parents' own self-reports, others will have been noticed independently by facilitators. The changes mentioned by the 51 respondents have been grouped as shown in Table 13.

The perceived changes for children are shown in Table 14 in the same way.

In assessing whether these changes were noticed immediately (that is, during or immediately after attendance at the programme) about half felt that for parents the changes were immediate (25 respondents) and were also longer lasting (30 respondents). Some people, not surprisingly, indicated that the outcome varied for different parents and children and it was impossible to give a simple answer to this question. A significant minority (eight) felt that for parents the changes were not long lasting, and that there was a danger that parents would, as one commented, 'fall back into their old ways'.

An examination of the links between reported changes for parents and for children indicates that in some cases increased confidence and self-esteem in parents was accompanied by

Table 13:   Changes in parents reported by scheme organisers/facilitators

Reported change	No. times mentioned (n=51)
Increase in self-confidence or self-esteem	18
Better understanding of own behaviour and of children's needs	10
Improved skills for parenting	10
Better parent-child relationships, more enjoyment of children	7
Feel more in control/assertive	7
Less anger, more calm	4
Less stress	3
Less depression	2
Better communication	2
Less smacking	2
Less isolated	1
Less guilt	1

Table 14:   Changes in children reported by scheme organisers/facilitators

Reported change	No. times mentioned (n=51)
Improvement in behaviour	10
Improved relationship/communication with parents	7
Less tension/stress/temper; quieter & calmer	7
Increase in self-esteem	6
More responsive, compliant, obedient	5
Happier, more cheerful	3
Better school performance	2
Able to express anger	1
Can play spontaneously	1
Show respectful assertiveness	1
More prepared to take responsibility for self	1

increased self-esteem in children; that calmer parents may have led to quieter children; that parents having more positive feelings about themselves might be linked to improved family relationships overall; that increased parental confidence was accompanied by a reduction in challenging behaviour in children.

Evaluations of programmes in the UK

Although there was very considerable anecdotal evidence about the success and effectiveness of all programmes in the survey, only 18 respondents indicated that the programme had been, or was in the process of being, externally evaluated. Written up or published evaluation reports, nine of which were undertaken externally, were available for 15 programmes (see Appendix II). Despite the variation in depth and objectivity of these evaluations, all without exception reported some positive changes in either parents or children, or both. Only one report noted a negative effect for just one parent. An analysis of these evaluations resulted in the identification of a number of themes.

All but one of these 15 evaluations were undertaken on different programmes, and on quite different bases, so that direct comparison is difficult. Six of them related to what have been described in Chapter 2 as 'behavioural' programmes and nine to similarly categorized 'relationships' programmes. In six instances, the author of the evaluation report was closely connected with the programme itself, either having been responsible for its development, training group leaders or leading the evaluated groups themselves. The remaining nine evaluation studies were undertaken externally. The scale of the evaluation studies, that is the number of individuals and/or the number of groups which formed the subjects of the research, was on the whole fairly small. Five studies involved a single implementation of a programme; the remainder covered at least one replication of the same programme, either going on in parallel, or at a later date. Nine studies involved fewer than 50 parents, and the scale ranged, for example, from six parents attending the Kidderminster Coping with Kids programme, to 107 expectant couples in the PIPPIN study. So far as the design of the studies was concerned, only four of the 14 used control groups (Managing Difficult Children, Behaviour Management Workshops, PIPPIN and Handling Children's Behaviour); the remainder focused on the intervention group only. For measurement of effect, a wide range of instruments was used across all the studies. Some form of parent self-report or self-completion questionnaire or parent interview was used by all studies, although this was the sole form of measure in only two of the 15. Pre- and post-test instruments were used in some form in nine of the evaluations, the remainder relying only on post-intervention reports.

In the group of six studies of 'behavioural' programmes, four were of the more rigorous type, using control groups or pre- and post-intervention measures, or both. The outcomes of these four, indicated improvements in parents' attitudes, skills and knowledge, and also in children's behaviour. Two of these specifically mentioned improvement in parents' self-esteem. The fifth, less rigorous, study also reported changes in children's behaviour and parents' attitude. The sixth study related to the link between attachment and parent change rather than to effect *per se*.

In the group of studies of 'relationships' programmes, regardless of the degree of rigour employed in the studies, there was much emphasis on increasing parents' self-confidence, self-esteem, sense of feeling valued and sense of empowerment – the affective outcomes. In addition, some studies pointed to the more practical outcomes, such as being able to solve problems, use new approaches to child management and develop better knowledge and understanding.

Overall, in examining these evaluation studies of parenting programmes, we would agree with the conclusions of Dembo (1985), referred to earlier in this chapter, that certain changes in parents' attitudes and/or in children's behaviour were evident. However, the quality and type of research procedures varied greatly among the studies, so much so that differences in the goals and in the methods of each approach affected not only the choice of evaluation instruments, but also the reported programme outcomes.

Why is evaluation so difficult?

This chapter has indicated that we still do not know enough about the effectiveness of parenting programmes, despite the wealth of anecdotal evidence and the practically universal praise from the parents who do participate in these programmes. But for policy makers, funders and others who must rely on a more rigorous approach to discovering the relationship between cause and effect, this is generally not sufficient evidence. This relationship is notoriously difficult to prove in any intervention in the social field. Why is this particularly so in the field of parenting programmes? We have already mentioned in this chapter some of the theoretical considerations involved – the range of different types of effectiveness which may need to be demonstrated, and the different perspectives which may be held about these. In addition to these theoretical considerations, there are also ethical, methodological, policy and resource matters to be thought about.

From an ethical standpoint, unless rigorous research methods are used, there may be an assumption that the intervention has an effect and, moreover, has no negative consequences. However, if it is decided to use a control group, is it then right to withhold the parenting programme from parents in that group? And again, if a control group is used (a waiting list group, for example), should participants be informed about the research and their allocation to different groups?

When thinking about the methodology to be used in the evaluation of a parenting programme, it is important to try to rule out alternative explanations for the outcome. This may prove difficult in the context of parenting programmes which aim to increase parents' self-confidence and self-esteem. For instance, a parent who gains enough confidence to make use of other community facilities, increases her/his social circle and that of her/his child, takes on responsibilities, and gets a job, is very likely to score highly on outcome measures. But what is the true causative agent? A further methodological difficulty is that the outcomes anticipated as a result of parenting programmes are not always easy to measure. Appendix II does, however, refer to a number of measurement instruments, many of them well-established, valid and reliable.

Finally, certain methodological approaches, for example the evaluation of a single series of parenting programme sessions, may make it impossible to make generalisations about the effectiveness of the programme. It may be that 'effect' only holds for a particular programme, at a particular time, with a certain group of participants, a particular facilitator and using a specific process.

Policy and resources issues are also important when considering the evaluation of parenting programmes. Testing the effectiveness of parenting programmes in a rigorous way is costly in terms of both time and money. This presents a dilemma for both policy makers and practitioners in terms of deciding whether to wait until the effects of each and every programme are definitively 'proven', or even until appropriate funds become available to commence such an evaluation, before introducing a programme when the need and the demand appear to be obvious.

Given the constraints and difficulties around the evaluation of parenting programmes, but nevertheless the importance of knowing what works, how it works, and for whom, it would seem that a balance needs to be found between time, cost and thoroughness of the evaluation.

Summary

This chapter has indicated that, in research terms, there are still a number of unanswered questions about the effectiveness of parenting programmes. Anecdotal evidence, parents' self-reporting and the views of a range of professionals all suggest positive outcomes for both parents and children, in terms of a number of indicators. There is still scope, however, for more long-term, controlled studies. There is also a need for regular, ongoing collection of data which can be used to add to the body of knowledge about these programmes. The suggestions in the following chapter may help in this regard.

7. A possible framework for evaluation

This chapter sets out some ideas and suggestions for practitioners wanting to evaluate their own programmes, or to commission an external evaluation. As the study progressed, it became evident that practioners would welcome help with monitoring and evaluation of parenting programmes. Some of these suggestions, particularly the preliminary diagnostic questions, are equally applicable for use by anyone embarking on an evaluation exercise. The structured way in which they are presented, however, should help people to work through their ideas in a logical sequence.

These suggestions are offered not as a definitive method or a 'recipe for evaluation', but rather as a set of preliminary ideas from which to start thinking. Feedback on the use of these ideas, and discussion in various forums, will hopefully suggest ways forward for the eventual development of good practice guidelines for the evaluation of parenting programmes.

The evaluation framework

The framework begins with a set of questions about the proposed evaluation – diagnostic questions whose answers will help the overall design of the evaluation.

The four main questions in the following self-completion framework are:

- Why evaluate?
- Who is interested in the outcome of the evaluation?
- What resources are available?
- Which outcomes should be measured?

The framework strategy then breaks into three sections (see page 106):

- management information;
- process information;
- outcome information.

Table 15:   Parenting Programmes:
A framework for evaluation

Preliminary questions

Questions	Answers
Why evaluate?	
Why is the evaluation needed?	
What pressure is there to evaluate, and where is it coming from?	
Is there pressure for any particular type of evaluation?	

This page may be reproduced for non-commercial circulation, subject to acknowledgement of source.

Questions	Answers
Who is interested in the outcome of the evaluation?	
Who wants to know about the effectiveness of the programme: parent participants, policy makers, funders, programme authors, facilitators, other practitioners, others?	
Which group's interests should take priority?	
Do these different groups of stakeholders require different information?	
Is it possible to design an evaluation which will meet the needs of all these stakeholders?	

What resources are available?				
What funding is available for evaluation?				
Is this sufficient? If not, where do we look for further funding?				
If no further funding is available, what does this mean for the scale and type of evaluation we can do?				
What time, resources are available, from practitioners, participants, outside researchers, and so on? Can we make full use of the data we collect?				

Questions	Answers		
What resources are available? (continued)			
Do we have access to researchers/evaluators who have the necessary knowledge and skills?			
Are there ways in which such people might assist with the evaluation, other than taking sole responsibility for it?			
Are there any previous evaluation reports which can be consulted for help in design?			

Which outcomes should be measured?			
What indicators of programme effectiveness are appropriate for this programme, and for the various stakeholders with an interest in the results?			
Which outcomes are likely to prove the most compelling to the various stakeholders?			
Which outcomes will provide us, and others, with information useful for programme development or repetition?			

A three-part strategy

I. Management information

Whether the programme being evaluated is intended for universal access, or is targeted to a particular group of parents, it will be necessary to know exactly who it is reaching, and also who, of its intended recipients, it is not reaching. So, from the start it is necessary to collect **initial data** about participants in a systematic way.

- Basic social and demographic characteristics
- Employment status
- Educational status
- Use of other community services
- How did participants hear about the programme?
- Why did participants enrol? (If participants were referred, this type of question also needs to be addressed to the referring agency.)
- What do participants hope to gain from attending?
- Attendance record
- Reasons for non-attendance or drop-out
- Name and address of contact through whom participant could be traced at a later date for a longer-term study.

II. Process information

This type of information will generally be recorded by group leaders or facilitators, and will focus on a descriptive record of how the programme works – that is, the actual processes involved. It might include, for example, such things as a brief evaluation of each session by the group leader, noting any particular helping relationships amongst participants, any useful learning mechanisms employed, any particular problems caused by individual participants, any particularly helpful problem-solving strategies used and any ideas for avoiding problems in the future.

III. Outcome information

This is perhaps the central core of any evaluation, and the one to which many people might jump directly, without proper consideration of the preliminary questions, or recognising the need to focus on other types of information too. Outcomes constitute just one part, albeit an important part, of an evaluation strategy. This is where the choices have to be made about which questions require answers, which measures will provide those answers, and which instruments are to be used to make those measurements. These choices are likely to vary for different programmes, for different audiences and for different evaluators. Examples of some of the outcomes which schemes may want to assess include the following:

- change in parents' attitudes to children and to parenting;
- change in parents' knowledge and understanding of behavioural principles;
- change in parents' self-esteem;
- change in parents' behaviour and parenting practice;
- change in children's behaviour;
- change in children's self-esteem.

Values and principles

The quality, effectiveness and usefulness of a parenting programme can be judged in part by whether it 'works' for its participants and their families, and the preceding sections have discussed formal evaluation studies, and also suggested ways in which this assessment can be approached by practitioners. However, there are other aspects of parenting programmes which constitute their quality, and we consider just two here – ethical principles and underpinning values.

Ethical principles

All work with families should operate within a framework of ethical principles, whereby families are fully aware of the objectives and methods of any intervention, and understand any requirements likely to be made of them. In the case of parenting programmes one way of doing this is to make available a set of information about the programme for participants and potential participants. A suggested checklist is as follows:

- description of the programme content;
- who the programme is for;
- the goals of the programme;
- methods used in the groups;
- the reasoning behind the methods;
- any research findings about the programme;
- any possible negative effects of the programme;
- group leaders: who they are, qualifications, training;
- freedom of choice for participants.

Underpinning values

Reference was made in Chapter 4 to the value base of parenting programmes, pointing out that no programme can be truly value-free. On the contrary, the integrity of a programme can be best understood by knowledge of the beliefs and values on which it is based. This book has emphasised the view that there is no blueprint for parenting and, therefore, no single parenting programme which will meet the needs of all parents. The diversity of family composition and of child rearing attitudes and practices need to be recognised in parenting programmes. Many of these ideas were discussed and elaborated by Professor Sheila Wolfendale (Professor of Psychology, University of East London) at a seminar which formed part of this study in March 1994.

The following table, listing a number of important underpinning values, is presented as a self-appraisal exercise. The intention is for practitioners to closely explore their practice and where possible to cite exact examples of programme *content* or *process* which clearly illustrates each of the aims listed in the left-hand column. This framework might be used in an ongoing way, with practitioners and parents going through the table at intervals, looking objectively to find examples of each underpinning value, or to work out ways of ensuring that they are incorporated in the future.

Table 16:   Parenting Programmes: A framework for self-appraisal

Underpinning values

Underpinning values	Example of programme content or process that promotes each aim	Achieved (A) Working on (W) Not yet included (N)
Incorporates multicultural family factors		
Actively challenges gender role, race and religious stereotyping		
Recognises and addresses socioeconomic differences and their influence upon parenting		

This page may be reproduced for non-commercial circulation, subject to acknowledgement of source.

Underpinning values	Example of programme content or process that promotes each aim	Achieved (A) Working on (W) Not yet included (N)
Welcomes and recognises a diversity of family composition		
Values and addresses diversity in child rearing attitudes and practices		
Operates a 'wealth' model of family heritage, rather than a 'deficit' model of family needs		
Promotes empowerment of parents to be in control of their lives		

Emphasises parents' existing skills		
Fosters the development of new skills for parents		
Explores what is meant by parental responsibility		
Addresses possible tension between children's and parents' rights		
Allows parents and group leaders to share their expertise on a basis of equality		

Underpinning values	Example of programme content or process that promotes each aim	Achieved (A) Working on (W) Not yet included (N)
Recognises the parenting role of people other than a child's birth parents		
Promotes an understanding of child development		
Promotes an understanding of relationships: couple, father-child, mother-child, child-child		
Actively welcomes feedback from parents and acts upon it		

This page may be reproduced for non-commercial circulation, subject to acknowledgement of source.

Summary

This chapter is rather different from the others in this book, in that it offers optional working exercises as a way in which practitioners can both begin to assess the quality of the parenting programme with which they are involved, and also design a system for evaluating its effectiveness. Both these tasks need to be seen as an on-going integral part of practice. Only thus can programmes develop and respond to parents' needs in a flexible way, yet do so within a structured framework.

8. Parenting programmes: the lessons learned

This final chapter summarises what we know about structured group-based parenting programmes in the UK as a result of this survey, highlights some of the issues raised by the study and the lessons which can be learned and applied in the development of parenting programmes. Finally, comment is made about some of the broader policy issues concerned with work in this area.

Summary

Within the broad area of support and education for parents, this survey has noted a considerable growth and interest in the more formal type of group-based parenting programme during the last five to ten years. Many of the programmes examined in the study have been developed during the 1990s, and more agencies and individuals are now interested in their use as a form of parent support for a wide range of parents.

Within the group of 38 programmes about which information was collected for the survey, many have multiple objectives but most are working towards supporting parents to become problem solvers, who understand the effects of their own behaviour on their children, and who feel confident and empowered in their role as parents. Three main groups of parents have been identified as taking part in these group-based programmes: those who want to do the best for their children, who want to be *good enough* parents, or who want to be affirmed in their parenting style; secondly, parents whose children exhibit behaviour problems of varying severity; and thirdly, parents who have multiple problems, including depression and extremely low self-esteem.

The programmes use a wide range of approaches and methods, but the 38 programmes examined divided themselves fairly equally into a group which aimed primarily to help parents to change their children's behaviour, and a group which aimed mainly to help parents change and improve communication and relationships within the family in a more in-depth way. Within these two groups there was further diversity of approach and use of the materials in order to be responsive to parents' particular needs. The approach adopted by the programmes tended to be founded on a range of theoretical principles. A number used social learning/behavioural principles as their main thrust; others were based more on family systems theory; many tended to adopt an eclectic mix of a number of different approaches and there was some evidence that eclecticism is sometimes taken to even greater lengths by mixing elements of different programmes, books and other resources to produce an end result which the programme developer considers appropriate for the needs of particular parents.

The survey found that the availability of parenting programmes tended to be patchy, and often dependent on the interest and enthusiasm of individuals or particular organisations. There was little evidence of a co-ordinated approach to the provision of parenting programmes on a local basis. As to the accessibility of programmes for parents, it would appear that the majority of those who are attracted to enrol are white, middle class women. Few fathers tend to be involved. Black families may not always find the approach of programmes appropriate for their cultural attitudes to parenting, and some programmes are not appropriate for those who are not comfortable with the written word. There was some evidence of attempts to address these challenges raised by sensitivity to the issues of class, gender and ethnicity, but more needs to be done to ensure that programmes are both accessible and available to all those parents who want them.

The range of organisations and individuals involved in promoting, funding and organising parenting groups is considerable. Amongst the statutory agencies, health authorities and trusts and local education authorities are the most prominent, with high input, too, from the voluntary sector. Amongst the individual professionals involved, educational psychologists and health visitors were most numerous, with social workers, teachers, nursery nurses, and parents themselves also involved. There was clear evidence that many of the programmes have begun their development in the UK through the

interest and enthusiasm of 'pioneer' figures, who have identified the need and gone on to develop an approach to meet it. The
degree of training undertaken by group leaders and group facilitators varied widely. Some were required to go through a selection process, followed by a fairly intensive training process,
whilst at the other extreme, parents who might have no specific
training were encouraged to become group leaders. For other
programmes, professional qualifications, such as educational
psychology were considered adequate for people leading
groups.

The actual materials used in these programmes ranged from
glossily published handbooks for both parents and group leaders (and often including supplementary videotape or audiotape
material), to simpler duplicated sheets and handouts. All fell
within the parameters of this study because of their ability to
be replicated with successive groups of parents. The majority of
the programmes were structured, in the sense that they were
made up of a series of sessions with topics or themes to be
covered on each occasion. Many were, however, used quite flexibly, with the order of sessions sometimes being altered, some
sessions being omitted, or the material being added to from
other sources.

An examination of the effectiveness of parenting programmes concluded that there was an absence of reliable data
on which to base firm judgments about the outcomes of the
majority of these programmes, for both parents and children.
There is a range of complex issues around the issue of the measurement of effectiveness which makes it difficult to determine
which approaches work best, and for which particular parents.
What was clear, however, was that parents' self-reports were
almost always enthusiastic, with many reporting change in
themselves and their children, or in improved family relationships more generally.

Learning points

This book has been written for those who are thinking of setting
up or organising some form of parenting programme in their
local area. Along the way, whilst reading each chapter, ideas
may have been generated, difficulties suggested themselves or
problems to avoid been noted. The aim of this next section is to
pull together some of the learning points which may have been
highlighted by this study. They are presented in the form of

diagnostic questions which will perhaps help course leaders and organisers to sort out their ideas and undertake some planning with colleagues and parents.

Why does the promotion of parenting programmes seem to be a good way forward?

This basic, but important, question may promote some discussion and self-examination about the purpose of parenting education in general and help organisers to be very clear in their own minds about the reasons for their involvement and the validity of the chosen approach.

Is there a demand for parenting programmes in this area?

It may be helpful to undertake some sort of 'needs survey', both among parents themselves and among professionals who might have identified a need or demand for such approaches in the course of their work. There have been examples of programmes being launched and publicised, but which have foundered because of apparent lack of interest. Perhaps there are other people in the area doing something similar, who would be willing to share their experiences, so that general local networking will be a useful process to go through.

If the demand is there, which sort of approach would be most appropriate?

If programme organisers are unfamiliar with these courses it will clearly be helpful to get to know something about them before making a definite decision. The descriptions in Chapters 2 and 5 will hopefully have begun to do this. Talking to people who have already had experience in this field may be one of the best ways. The contacts listed in the Appendix I and Appendix III may help. Local libraries and health promotion agencies may be able to help. The needs survey may also indicate whether parents in the area are interested in the more in-depth approach helping with improving family relationships, or whether they have identified behaviour difficulties which they would like to understand how to change.

What about facilitator training?

Is it possible to locate trained facilitators (via a local Parent-Link organisation, for example?) Are there ways in which groups of potential facilitators can be trained? What ongoing support can we build in for group leaders? Leading a parent group of this sort can be complex and difficult, even when the programme itself provides plenty of guidance or even, as in the case of the Family Caring Trust programmes, there is a complete text for leaders to make use of. Issues can arise, or tensions develop, which may need careful and sensitive handling, so that facilitators should always have someone with whom they can discuss problems and de-brief after group sessions.

What about practical arrangements?

Funding, venue, crèche provision, day of the week, time of day, cost to participants, refreshments, materials, handouts, audio-visual equipment, furnishings and layout of the room: all these are important practical points which may need extensive forward planning. Care and attention to detail at this point is likely to pay off later. The needs survey may indicate parents' preferences over timing, day of the week and provision of a crèche or other form of family support.

How can parents' be involved in the planning of the course?

Time and again in this book there has been an emphasis on the need to begin from parents' own needs and parents' own strengths. There should, therefore, be a way of parents being able to contribute to the course content, even when a very structured programme is being used. Facilitators need to know which topics or themes or examples of problems parents expect to cover, and can then ensure that provision is made for this.

What is the best way to publicise the course?

There is probably no single best way of doing this, since each and every community is different, and some participants may be referred through other agencies so that generalised publicity is not appropriate. Many programmes have found that holding a well-publicised information session about the programme gives parents an opportunity to decide whether it is for them, whether they can make such a commitment, whether they can afford it, and so on. This is where the ethical principles referred to in Chapter 7 can be incorporated, by having information available along the lines suggested on p.107.

What about monitoring or evaluation?

The arguments in favour of evaluation, including a suggested model for evaluation and a framework for self-evaluation of the underlying principles incorporated in the programme, are set out in Chapter 7. It is essential that this aspect of the programme is given due consideration at a very early stage of planning and that it is developed alongside the sessions themselves as an integral part of the course. Even if a decision is taken not to conduct a rigorous outcome evaluation at this point, it will not be difficult to set up systems for collecting, recording and analysing the management information and process information suggested.

Policy implications

In Chapter 1, a number of reasons were suggested for the growing interest in the support which parents need in order to do the best for their children – the point from which almost all parents start. There is, however, still debate about whether parenting takes place entirely within a private domain (the family) or whether, partly at least, it is perceived as being in the public domain. There have been a number of calls for *all* parents to have access to appropriate preparation, education and support at relevant stages in their parenting life. Recognition of the needs of all parents in this way brings the whole issue clearly into the public domain where the state has a role to play.

However, despite the intentions of the Children Act 1989, which assumed that resources could, and would, be redirected towards preventative work, including parent education and support, the fact is that the major share of resources is still being targeted at a small number of families with children defined as being 'in need'. There is still no national policy on education and support for parents, neither is there much evidence of local co-ordination of such services across statutory and voluntary sectors.

This book has suggested that, in order to be responsive to the diverse needs of parents, there should be a similarly diverse range of approaches and methods available for parent education and support, both generally and within the particular group-based approach which is the subject of this book. Although this does add to the difficulty of developing a national policy for universal parent education, it is nevertheless important in responding to a rationale for parenting education programmes. If the aim of parent education is to give individual parents the means to increase their self-confidence and give them control over their own lives, then there must be a range of programmes delivered in a style which is relevant and appropriate to their individual needs, socioeconomic status, ethnicity, gender and class.

This issue of diversity is closely tied up with the availability of programmes and their accessibility to parents. Increased availability can really only be achieved by means of increased resources, so that in any local community, parents should be able to locate a range of programmes in order to find the one which is appropriate for their own individual needs. Accessibility is perhaps more complex. To start with, there needs to be a recognition that it is normal and usual to attend such programmes – no stigma should attach to parents who ask for or seek help of this kind at various stages of their parenting career. Programmes need to be *perceived* as being accessible – that is, parents need to be convinced of their value and relevance to their particular needs. And finally, the more practical aspects of accessibility such as location, cost and time of day need to be carefully considered and agreed with members of local communities.

A further issue emerging from this study is about who should run, and who should pay for, parenting programmes. The survey has shown that a wide range of professionals are now involved in this particular group-based approach, but for many this is not yet a part of their mainstream work. If availability and accessibility are to be improved, then such work does need to become mainstream, and to take place in places which parents tend to use – schools, nurseries, health clinics and so on.

There are messages here for those involved in the initial training, and in-service training, of teachers, midwives, health visitors and so on. As yet there seems little agreement about exactly what, or how much, training is required to lead parenting course groups, but there is more consensus about which skills facilitators need to have, or to acquire through training.

The study has suggested that many of the people developing and organising parenting programmes have tended, hitherto, to be somewhat isolated. Dissemination, networking and discussion therefore must become more widespread to avoid too much reinvention of the wheel. This book is just one contribution to that increased interaction and communication.

References

Adler, D (1927) *Understanding human nature* US, New York: Greenberg Publishing.

Adler, D (1930) *The Education of Children.* US, New York: Greenberg Publishing.

Allan, J (1994) 'Parenting education in Australia', *Children & Society*, 8, 4, 344-359.

Audit Commission (1994) *Seen But Not Heard: developing community child health and social services for children in need.* HMSO.

Baginsky, M (1993) *Parent Link in Waltham Forest: an evaluation.* Baginsky Associates for Waltham Forest LEA.

Bavolek, S (1990) 'Parenting: theory, policy and practice', *Research and Validation Report of the Nurturing Programmes.* US Wisconsin: Eau Claire.

Berne, E (1964) *Games People Play.* US, New York: Grove Press.

Berne, E (1973) *What do you say after you say hello?* US, New York: Bantam Books.

Bradley, H and Weller, M (1994) *Coping with Kids: an evaluation of a parenting group.* Kidderminster: unpublished.

Brim, O (1959) *Education for child rearing* US, New York: Russell Sage.

Cannan, C (1992) *Changing Families, Changing Welfare.* Harvester Wheatsheaf.

Clench, H (1994) 'Empowering parents of children with special educational needs'. Unpublished paper presented at the International Conference 'Empowering People in Families, Plymouth.

Cocks, R (1994) *Parent education courses and an analysis of educational psychologists' involvement.* Unpublished dissertation for MSc. Psychology Department, University of East London.

Coping with Kids (1994) Annual Report 1993-1994. Coping with Kids.

Cooper, C '"Good enough", borderline and "bad enough" parenting', *in* Adcock, M and White, R (1985) *Good Enough Parenting: a framework for assessment*. British Association for Adoption and Fostering.

Crisp, S (1994) *Counting on Families: social audit report on the provision of family support services*. Exploring Parenthood.

Davies, E (1978) 'An evaluation of packaged parent education programs', *Aust Journal of Social Issues*, 13,3,187-196.

Dawson, J (1995) *Positive Parenting: an evaluation*. Postgraduate School of Psychology, University of Nottingham.

Dembo, M, Sweitzer, M and Lauritzen, P (1985) 'An Evaluation of Group ParentEducation: Behavioural, PET and Adlerian Programmes', *Review of Educational Research*, 55, 2, pp 155-200.

Dinkmeyer, D and McKay, G (1976) *Systematic training for effective parenting*. American Guidance Service. Circle Pines, Minnesota, USA.

Dinkmeyer, D and McKay, G (1982) *The Parents' Handbook – Systematic Training for Effective Parenting*. American Guidance Service. Circle Pines, Minnesota, USA.

Doherty, W and Ryder, R (1980) 'Parent Effectiveness Training (PET): criticisms and caveats', *J. Marital & Family Therapy*, 6,4,409-419.

Dreikurs, R and Soltz, V (1964) *Happy Children: a challenge to parents*. US, New York: Hawthorn.

Dreikurs, R and Soltz, V (1964) *Children: the challenge*. US, New York: Hawthorn.

Edwards, J (1995) '"Parenting skills": views of community health and social service providers about the needs of their "clients".' *Jnl Soc Pol, 24, 2, 237-259*.

Edwards, E and Townsend, L (1993) *Working with Parents for Change*. Strathclyde Regional Council.

Eyken, van der, W (1992) *Introducing Evaluation*, Bernard van Leer Foundation.

Finch, G (1994) *Handling Children's Behaviour*. NCH Action for Children.

Fine, M (1980) *ed. Handbook on Parent Education*. Academic Press, USA.

Fine, M (1989) *ed. The second handbook on parent education*. Academic Press, USA.

Gordon, T (1975) *Parent Effectiveness Training.* New York: Peter Wyden.

Harman, D and Brim, O (1980) *Learning to be parents: principles, programmes and methods.* Sage.

Hartley-Brewer, E and Hills, L (1994) *Effective Parenting: Facilitator's Manual.* E Hartley-Brewer and L Hills (copies available from the authors).

Hearn, B (1995) *Child and family support and protection: a practical approach.* National Children's Bureau.

Hewitt, K and others (1991) 'Parent education in preventin behaviour problems', *Health Visitor,* 64, 12.

Hinton, S (1988) *A Study of Behaviour Management Workshops for Parents of Nursery School Children.* A report submitted for an Associateship at the Institute of Education, University of London.

Holman, R (1992) 'Family Centres', *Highlight No. 111.* National Children's Bureau.

Jones, P (1994) *Parentwise: project description, October 1994,* Parentwise, Plymouth.

Katz, A (1994) 'The family is fine...but under pressure', Sainsbury's Magazine, May 1994.

Lawes, G (1992) 'Individual parent training implemented by nursery nurses: evaluation of a programme for mothers of pre-school children. *Behavioural Psychotherapy* 20, 239- 256.

McGaw, S (1993) 'The Special Parenting Service – supporting parents with learning difficulties' *Disability, Pregnancy and Parenthood International* 4, 8-10.

McGaw, S (1994) 'Assessing parents with learning disabilities: the parental skills model' *Child Abuse Review* 3, 1, 1-16.

McGaw, S (1995) *I want to be a good parent.* (Set of 5 booklets: What's it like to be a parent? Children need healthy food. Children need to be clean, healthy and warm. Children need to be safe. Children need love.) Kidderminster: British Institute of Learning Disabilities.

Medway, F (1989) 'Measuring the effectiveness of parent education'. Chapter 10 in Fine, M ed (1989) *The second handbook of parent education.* USA, Academic Press.

Miller, S (1994) *Positive Parenting.* Learning Materials Development Consultancy.

Neville, D, King, L and Beak, D (1995) *Promoting Positive Parenting.* Areno.

Parr, M (1994) An innovative intervention for British couples in the transition to parenthood. PhD thesis (in preparation).

Patterson, G and Narrett, C (1990) 'The development of a reliable and valid treatment programme for aggressive young children' *International Journal of Mental Health* 19, 3, 19-26.

Penny, F (1994) *Final evaluation: report of Positive Parenting project*. Faculty of Social Sciences, University of Northumbria.

Puckering, C, Rogers, J, Mills, M, Cox, A D, Mattsson-Graff, M (1994) 'Process and evaluation of a group intervention for mothers with parenting difficulties' *Child Abuse Review*, 3, pp 299-310.

Pugh, G (1994) *Effective Parenting Programme for Schools: A pilot study*. National Children's Bureau.

Pugh, G, De'Ath, E and Smith, C (1994) *Confident Parents, Confident Children: policy and practice in parent education and support*. National Children's Bureau.

Redpath, R (1991) *Pre-school intervention: an evaluation*. Renfrew Division Psychological Service, Strathclyde Region.

Roberts, C and others (1995) *Parenting Problems: a national study of parents and parenting problems*. Family Policy Studies Centre.

Rogers, C (1951) *Client-centred therapy*. US, Boston: Houghton-Mifflin.

Rogers, C R (1961) *On becoming a person: a therapist's view of psychotherapy*. US, Boston: Houghton Mifflin.

Routh, C, Hill, J, Steele, H, Elliott, C and Dewey, M (1994) 'Maternal attachment status, psychosocial stressors and problem behaviour: follow-up after parent training courses for conduct disorder' In press.

Rylands, J (1995) *A study of parenting programmes in Ireland: exploration of needs and current provision*. Barnardo's and Department of Health.

Schlossman, S (1976) 'The parent education game: the politics of child psychology in the 1970s. *Teachers' College Record*, 79.

Schmidt Neven, R (1990) *The New Explorers: a psychodynamic approach to parenting in a changing society*. Full Circle. London.

Sutton, C (1992) 'Training parents to manage difficult children: a comparison of methods'. *Behavioural Psychotherapy*, 20, 115-139.

Utting, D (1995) *Family and Parenthood: supporting families, preventing breakdown.* Joseph Rowntree Foundation.

Utting, D, Bright, J and Henricson, C (1993) *Crime and the Family: improving child-rearing and preventing delinquency.* Family Policy Studies Centre.

Webster-Stratton, C, Hollingsworth, T and Kolpacoff, M (1989) 'The long-term effectiveness and clinical significance of three cost-effective training programs for families with conduct-problem children', *Journal of Consulting and Clinical Psychology*, 57, 4, pp 550-553.

Wolfendale, S (1992) *Empowering Parents and Teachers: working for children.* Cassell

Winnicott, D (1964) *The Child, the Family and the Outside World.* Penguin.

Appendix I

Profiles of parenting skills programmes

ABC of Behaviour

Contact: Sonya Hinton
                       Educational Psychologist
                       Andrews House
                       College Road
                       Guildford GU1 4QF   01483 572881

Description: All parents find themselves from time to time not knowing 'what to do' about their children's difficult behaviour. The ABC booklet and workshops help parents work out their own solutions to everyday problems. The booklet explains the behavioural approach in straightforward everyday language with amusing illustrations. It offers examples of problems that many parents encounter and gives clear instructions on how to follow an ABC (antecedents, behaviour and consequences) of change so that more acceptable behaviour results. Five-session workshops following the format of the booklet but using parents' own problems have been running in Surrey since 1982.

Funding: Surrey Educational Psychology Service

Materials: Hinton, S (1993) *The ABC of Behaviour – troubleshooting for parents of young children*. Surrey County Council.

                       Hinton, S and Taylor, A (1993) *Right from the Start*. Surrey County Council.

Theoretical base: Social learning/behavioural.

Leader training: Training for facilitators provided by Sonya Hinton and Graham King.

Outcomes: Number of behaviour difficulties as reported by mothers and teachers decreases; parents' knowledge of behavioural strategies increases.

Evaluation: *A Study of Behaviour Management Workshops for Parents of Nursery School Children*. A report submitted for an associateship at the Institute of Education, University of London, by Sonya Hinton, 1986-87.

Publications: Materials as listed above.

Black Families Talking

Contact:	Lynthia Grant Exploring Parenthood 4 Ivory Place 20A Treadgold Street London W11 4PB 0171 221 4471
Description:	This project started as the Moyenda Project in 1992 and was set up to explore the needs of black parents with regard to support, information and counselling in parenting, and to prepare materials which respond to these needs. The project also organises parent support groups working with both African Caribbean and Asian families; and intends to produce relevant support materials, for example, leaflets and video materials, which could be used by parents, health visitors and social workers in addressing the concerns of black parents. About 150 parents have attended the programme so far.
Funding:	Department of Health.
Materials:	
Theoretical base:	Psychoanalytic.
Leader training:	Group work course.
Outcomes:	Parents feel more self-worth and have more self-confidence.
Evaluation:	No external evaluation. Written up in Moyenda Report.
Publications:	Article in *Nursery World*. Moyenda Report.

Coping with Kids (Assertive Discipline for Parents)

Contact: Behaviour Management Ltd
The Old Rectory
High Street
Iron Acton
Bristol BS17 1UQ   01454 228962
Tonia Robinson
Educational Psychologist
Merrywood Boys School
Daventry Road
Knowle, Bristol BS4 1QQ   0117 963 4965

Description: **Coping with Kids** is the British adaptation of Lee Canter's Assertive Discipline for Parents, published in the USA in 1985. There are three two-hour sessions which focus on the skills of staying calm, taking control and enjoying family life. The materials and activities have been adapted to meet the needs of parents living in deprived city areas in the UK as well as parents from more affluent backgrounds. Some 25 workshops have been run in Avon since 1992, based in various centres including schools, health clinics, Social Services Department day nurseries, workplace or private nurseries, church and community centres. The aim of the programme is to effect initial changes within the family system, through increasing parents' skills, confidence and self-esteem.

Funding: Safer Cities, Community Education, Avon Psychology Service

Materials: Canter, L and Canter, M (1988) *Assertive Discipline for Parents*. USA. Harper Row.
Canter, L and Canter, M (1985) *Parent Resource Guide*. Lee Canter and Associates Inc.

Theoretical base: Humanistic, social learning/behavioural, solution-focused.

Leader training: One-day leader training course including Leader's Manual, video and presentation materials supplied by Behaviour Management Ltd.

Outcomes: For parents: calmer, no shouting, positive statements, don't get into arguments, feel more in control, happier. For children: less inclined to argue, beginning to do as they are told, quieter, more cheerful.

Evaluation: Questionnaire feedback from parents; attendance and course records; leader's evaluation.

Publications: A range of books and materials available through Behaviour Management Ltd.

Coping with Kids (Kidderminster)

Contact: Mary Weller
Community Health Worker
Helen Bradley, Psychologist
Woodbury Centre
20 Woodbury Road
Kidderminster
DY11 7JL   01562 748406

Description: The materials used in this programme have been developed by the workers themselves. Six weekly sessions deal with different issues which have been highlighted by the parents, for example, play, smacking, food and sleep refusal. The parents' needs are explored in the first session and the topics included in the programme in the chosen order of priority. Children's rights issues are acknowledged as of primary importance. It is also openly acknowledged that families may have different beliefs, and the emphasis is to respect different mores. Three groups a year have been run since 1994, with 10-12 parents in each group.

Funding: National Health Service

Materials: The materials have been developed by the workers in the Woodbury Centre.

Theoretical base: Humanistic; social learning/behavioural; family systems; eclectic.

Leader training: Professional knowledge of child development and parenting skill needs, plus groupwork skills training.

Outcomes: For parents: more control of situations, less spontaneous anger, awareness that children are not deliberately being 'naughty'.

For children: less tense, more interaction with mother, receive fewer smacks.

Evaluation: One group written up. Changes in parents' confidence and enjoyment of their parenting.

Day Group Programme

Contact:	Pauline Mayes Child Therapist Manager of Day Unit – Under 8s Child and Family Guidance Wyvern Clinic Theatre Square Swindon SN1 1QN 01793 642666
Description:	This programme is for parents referred to the Child Mental Health Services, or parents may refer themselves. About 150 parents attend per year and the programme has been running since 1982. The objectives of the programme are to improve the parents' confidence in their ability to successfully parent their children. The materials are specifically designed by the professionals.
Funding:	Swindon and Marlborough Health Trust.
Materials:	Specially designed.
Theoretical base:	Social learning/behavioural.
Leader training:	Professional training and supervision. All staff either psychology graduate or teaching background.
Outcomes:	Parents are more confident, increase in self-esteem, calmer. Improvement in play skills. Children are more compliant.
Evaluation:	No external evaluation. Results written up.
Publications:	None so far, but the group programme was presented at a national conference in 1990.

Effective Parenting

Contact: Janet Muscutt
                       Educational Psychologist
                       Bewsey Old School
                       Lockton Lane
                       Bewsey
                       Warrington   01925 44144 (Work)
                                                     01925 602769 (Home)

Description: This programme is operated by Cheshire County Psychological Service, with about 60 parents attending during 1994. Its objectives are to assist parents in being clear about what behaviours they want from their children; what behaviours are developmentally appropriate; how to effectively reinforce those behaviours. This programme is targetted on preschool children. The County also offers Canter's Assertive Parenting course for children of all ages.

Funding: Cheshire Under-8s Forum.

Materials: Drawn from various sources.

Theoretical base: Social learning/behavioural; family systems.

Leader training: Educational psychologist trains others.

Outcomes: Parents feed back their experiences of trying out their action plans between sessions and report on their children's responses and reactions.

Evaluation: None so far. Programme still being developed.

Effective Parenting

Contact:	Elizabeth Hartley-Brewer 117 Corringham Road London NW11 7DL 0181 458 8404 Larraine Hills 84 Ridgeview Road London N20 0HL 0181 445 6487

Description: This is a primary school-based programme offered by schools designed to support parents in their parenting role; to provide a forum to share experiences, fears and anxieties; to pool practical tips; to develop better understanding of relationships and behaviour and the stages of child development. It is intended to bridge the gap between home and school, and to raise both parents' and children's self-esteem. Sixteen schools (236 parents) participated in a pilot in 1993/94. A further 36 schools were involved in 1994/95. Topics include Discipline, Sibling Rivalry, Stress & the family, TV & Video games, Play, Security vs. Independence, Starting School, Lying and Stealing.

Funding: LEAs and schools.

Materials: The Effective Parenting 'Facilitators' Manual' contains detailed guidelines for running the 12 topics, and includes handouts for parents for each topic.

Theoretical base: Humanistic; social learning/behavioural; eclectic.

Leader training: Accompanying eight-session training course (16 hours total) Facilitating Parent Groups. Training for school personnel in groupwork skills, preparation, use of media, conceptual framework. Cascade training is also available, supported by a detailed Leaders' Manual.

Outcomes: For parents: greater confidence, understanding and skills to fulfil their parenting role; closer rapport with school. For children: taking greater responsibility for their behaviour; better behaviour in classroom; fewer referrals to support service. For schools: enhanced status and confidence for teachers and others as result of leading groups.

Evaluation: External evaluation by Gillian Pugh (1994) *Effective Parenting Programme for Schools: a pilot study*. National Children's Bureau.

Publications: Articles: Independent 10.2.94; Education 10.6.94; TES 23.9.94; *Young Minds* Newsletter 9.94. Materials as above.

Everyday Problems in Childhood (EPIC)

Contact:
Hugh Clench
Senior Educational Psychologist
17 Hove Park Villas
Hove
East Sussex BN3 6HH   01273 675331 (Work)
01273 728375 (Home)

Description:
EPIC is an open learning course for all parents of children aged five and under, being concerned with those problems that all parents encounter from time to time. It aims to improve the quality of life for both parents and children. Approximately 100 parents attend the programme per year, since 1989. The programme is offered through playgroups, pre-school units etc. There is a version for parents of children with special educational needs which has a different introduction.

Funding:
Self-financing by sales of materials and fees.

Materials:
The EPIC materials are published by The Parent Company, and consist of 12 topics, five of which are general, and the remainder address specific problems. Presented in both printed and audiotape format, for parents with poor literacy skills.

Theoretical base:
Social learning/behavioural. The programme is not prescriptive and does not provide set answers.

Leader training:
Specific training not offered, although the materials include notes for group leaders. Leaders are normally people who have participated in a previous EPIC group, and who have good listening skills. There is a telephone helpline for group leaders, and additional noted for special needs group leaders. Specific training is available if requested.

Outcomes:
For parents: greater awareness and understanding of their children's needs; some specific problems solved; powerful feelings of empowerment especially among parents of children with special needs. For children: parents report that some problems have been solved.

Evaluation:
Written up. Both affective and practical outcomes found for parents of children with special needs.

Publications:
Nursery World, April 1990. Several papers presented at national and international conferences.
Empowering parents of children with special educational needs. Paper presented at ISEC 95, the 4th International Special Education Congress, Birmingham, 10-13 April 1995.

Family Caring Trust

Contact: Michael Quinn
                     Director
                     Family Caring Trust
                     44 Rathfriland Road
                     Newry
                     Co Down BT34 1LD   01693 64174

Description: The parenting programmes developed by the Family
                     Caring Trust are described as easy-to-run, flexible,
                     self-help courses for small groups of parents. There
                     are instructions for each session, including audio or
                     videotapes presenting typical family situations. The
                     objectives are to enable parents to communicate bet-
                     ter with their children and develop a growing sense of
                     responsibility in their children. Courses are organised
                     by schools, health visitors, churches and other com-
                     munity groups. The authors of this range of pro-
                     grammes, intended to provide support at all stages of
                     the family life cycle, have sold 1.7 million copies
                     worldwide. It is estimated that almost 200,000 par-
                     ents in the UK have experienced these courses since
                     1986.

Funding: Sales of materials, plus some support from DH and
                     voluntary organisations in development of some pro-
                     grammes.

Materials: Five main programmes: *Basic Parenting; Noughts to
                     sixes; Teen Parenting; Parent Assertiveness; Parenting
                     and Sex.* Each has a participants' handbook and
                     leaders' guide.

Theoretical base: Family systems, humanistic, social learning, with
                     Adlerian and Rogerian influences.

Leader training: Mainly hands-on experience of running groups on an
                     apprenticeship model.

Outcomes: Breaking unthinking patterns of parenting; more lis-
                     tening, communication and effective discipline. For
                     children: more communication, greater sense of
                     responsibility and autonomy.

Evaluation: No formal evaluation.

Publications: Various. Own newsletter. Health Visitor (1993) 66,
                     285. TES

Family Nurturing Network

Contact:

Annette Mountford
Ivana Klimes
Project Co-ordinators
Bernwood Annexe
Bernwood First School
Northway
Headington
Oxford OX3 9EU   01865 744566

Description: The Nurturing Programme is a course for groups of families It aims to promote positive parenting and nurturing skills throughout the family and to prevent and reduce physical and emotional abuse and neglect. The programme consists of 15 weekly sessions, with children and adults separately tackling similar topics at their appropriate levels, such as praise, anger, child development.

Funding: Joseph Rowntree Foundation.

Materials: *Nurturing Program for Parents and Children* by Stephen Bavolek and Christine Comstock (1993) published by the Family Development Resource, Utah, USA. There are several handbooks and leaders' manuals.

Theoretical base: Eclectic.

Leader training: 16-hour foundation training. Apprentice leaders then participate in one children's programme prior to pairing with trained leader as adult facilitator.

Outcomes: For parents: increased self-esteem; improved parenting skills and confidence; finding jobs; enabling other parents. For children: increased self-esteem; improved learning at school; decrease in temper, soiling, bullying, being bullied.

Evaluation: A number of measures are used before and after the 15 weeks (depression, attitude, self-esteem, personal evaluation, nurturing quiz, parenting skills) but the results have not been written up.

Goal Planning Course

Contact:　　　　　　Educational Psychology Service
13 Tetherdown
London
N10 1ND　　　　　　　　　　　0181 883 1094

Description:　　　　Parenting courses run in the London Borough of
Haringey by Educational Psychologists with mem-
bers of the Home Intervention Team (HINTS) specifically for parents of children with special educational
needs. The focus is particularly on behviour management and covered topics such as temper tantrums,
communication, sleeping and toileting.

Funding:　　　　　LB of Haringey

Theoretical base:　Social learning/behavioural

Leader training:　Leaders are trained Educational Psychologists

Handling Children's Behaviour

Contact: Graham Finch
Cornerstone Family Centre
NCH Action for Children
Howard Street
Hillfields Coventry   01203 256611

Other contacts: Freda Griggs   01926 495321 X 4044
Eileen Woodfield   01203 591619
Liz Dodds   01788 579488

Description: This programme was written by Graham Finch while he was working as a social worker in Child Guidance in Coventry. The leaders' manual has now been published by NCH Action for Children, and the programme is widely used in Coventry, Warwickshire, areas of·Birmingham and many other parts of the country. It is used in day nurseries and family centres, and has also been adapted for use with parents of children with special needs. The course usually consists of ten weekly sessions of two hours duration. Every effort is made to make the sessions relaxed, fun and educative rather than threatening to parents.

Funding: NCH Action for Children funded the publication, but the groups in operation are funded by various agencies.

Materials: *Handling Children's Behaviour* by Graham Finch (1994), published by NCH Action for Children.

Theoretical base: Social learning/behavioural.

Leader training: Apprentice model and cascade model (4 x 2hr sessions).

Outcomes: For parents: more confidence to take control, understanding children better. For children: calmer, happier, better relationship with parents.

Evaluation: External evaluation as comparison with individual parent training (see below).

Publications: Lawes, G (1992) 'Individual parent training implemented by nursery nurses: evaluation of a programme for mothers of pre-school children' *Behavioural Psychotherapy* 20, pp 239-256.

Help! I'm a Parent

Contact:	Tim Hollingdale Projects Manager Church Pastoral Aid Society (CPAS) Athena Drive Tachbrook Park Warwick CV34 6NG 01926 334242
Description:	This is a video-based training course. The kit consists of a ring binder including handouts, information, exercises and ways of running parenting groups, together with two video tapes giving nearly two hours of programmes, and a 160-page book. There are course outlines for parents of different age groups and the courses last for seven sessions (but can be adapted to be longer or shorter).
Funding:	Usually by local churches who buy the kit.
Materials:	The kit as described above costs £89.95. 750 were sold in the first six months.
Theoretical base:	Christian value base.
Leader training:	None, but the kit contains advice on leading groups.
Outcomes:	Not yet monitored.
Evaluation:	None so far.
Publications:	As described above.

Living with Teenagers

Contact:	Sonya Hinton Educational Psychologist Education Office Andrews House College Road Guildford GU1 4QF 01483 572881

Description: This is a course developed for parents of teenage children and run through schools in Surrey. Publicity is sent to all parents of Years 8 and 9 children. Three programmes per year have been run since 1993, each with four sessions. The objectives of the programme are for parents to develop an understanding of the life tasks of the teenage years, listening skills, different parenting styles, dealing with conflict and negotiation skills.

Funding: Surrey County Council Education Department.

Materials: Various sources are used. For example, *Working Together* (1980) by Helen Shaw and David Matthews; *Help, I've got a teenager* by Bayer and Bayer. Exley Pub.; Family Caring Trust Programme.

Theoretical base: Eclectic.

Leader training: Only one educational psychologist at the moment, though another is acting as observer and co-presenting courses in preparation for leading.

Outcomes: For parents: reported improved relationships with teenagers, and improved marital relationships. Very positive feedback. For young people: reported that mothers were more relaxed.

Evaluation: Evaluation sheet completed by parents at the end of the course.

Managing children with Asperger Syndrome and attention-deficit disorders

Contact: Lisa Blakemore-Brown
Chartered Educational Psychologist
22 King's Drive
Pagham
West Sussex PO21 4PY   01243 265389

Description: This programme has been used since 1993 with carers within a residential school environment. The intention is to introduce it to parents in the future. There are two or three sessions in each course and the objective is to inform and empower the carers in good 'parenting' skills with this specific group of children. It covers ways of managing the environment to reduce strain; understanding the child; development of non-aversive approaches and their importance; the importance of self-esteem and the need to develop self-efficacy in the children.

Funding: Hesley Group paid for initial training of carers. Now self-funded.

Materials: Materials developed for the purpose by the organiser, and also parts of other programmes, for example, *Building Self Esteem in Your Child* by Susan Baile; *Positive Approaches to Behaviour Change* by Warren and Hoffman. *Progress without Punishment – the use of non-aversive approaches* by Donnellan and Lavigna.

Theoretical base: Social learning/behavioural; eclectic.

Leader training: Professional qualifications and experience.

Outcomes: For parents: more positive, proactive, less stressed. More confident with better understanding and more skills. For children: behaviour improved, in some dramatically.

Evaluation: None so far. Under discussion with Portsmouth University.

Publications: None so far. In preliminary discussions with NFER Nelson.

Mellow Parenting

Contact:
Maggie Mills
Clinical Psychologist
2 Meard Street
London W1V 3HR   0171 287 6295

Christine Puckering
Clinical Psychologist
Glasgow University Dept of Psychological Medicine
Gartnavel Royal Hospital
Glasgow G12 0XH   0141 211 3920

Description: This is an intensive parenting intervention, with three linked components. The four-month group based package includes psychotherapy, and direct and video work with mothers and children using a multidimensional model of parenting. The programme is based in family centres in Scotland and the Child Psychiatry Day Unit at Guy's Hospital, London and has been operating since 1990. Some 36 parents per year attend the programme.

Funding: National Health Service, social work department, Barnardo's, Abelour Child Care Trust.

Materials: Own programme, developed 'in house'.

Theoretical base: Social learning/behavioural; psychoanalytic; attachment theory.

Leader training: The social workers, psychologists and psychiatrists, OTs, nurses, crèche workers etc who lead the programme receive initial and ongoing training. Initial training workshops are now organised approximately six-monthly.

Outcomes: In a pilot study of 21 mothers there was considerable positive change in interaction and child-centredness. Negative interaction dropped to one quarter of the pre-group level. Ten of 12 children on child protection register had their names removed.

Evaluation: Pilot study as described above, using observational data from pre- and post-group videotapes, anonymous feedback of self-report measures, and deregistration from the Child Protection Register. A larger Department of Health funded study with a control group and twelve month follow up is in progress.

Publications: Puckering, C, Rogers, J, Mills, M and Cox, A D (1994) 'Process and Evaluation of a Group Intervention for mothers with Parenting Difficulties' *Child Abuse Review* 3, 299-310.

NEWPIN

Contact:
Anne Jenkins or
Helen Jacey
National NEWPIN
Sutherland House
35 Sutherland Square
Walworth
London SE17 3EE   0171 703 6326
                                    (Fax) 0171 701 2660

Description:
NEWPIN is a national voluntary organisation whose objective is to help parents under stress to break the cyclical effect of destructive family behaviour. NEW-PIN offers parents and children a unique opportunity to achieve positive changes in their lives and relationships, based on respect, support, equality and empathy.

Funding:
National NEWPIN mainly by DH. Local NEWPIN Centres 75% statutory funding, plus trusts.

Materials:
The NEWPIN Personal Development Programme has three modules: Parent Skills Training; Family Play Programme; Learning for Life.

Theoretical base:
Humanistic, social learning/behavioural, psychoanalytic, family systems, eclectic, feminist.

Leader training:
The PDP is led by the NEWPIN Centre Co-ordinator and Family Play Facilitator, most of whom have previously attended NEWPIN Centres as parents in distress and subsequently as centre paid workers. NEWPIN provides in-service and induction training for staff. Some service users join NVQ programmes.

Outcomes:
External research has shown that the firmer the attachment to a NEWPIN Centre, the greater the positive changes in the mental health of the parent are likley to be. The modular programme with its emphasis on emotional growth for the parents and the parent/child relationship brings about a greater understanding of the child's need for nurture and support. Parents themselves believe that the relationships with their children have improved after participating in the programmes. Evaluation to date suggests that with sustained involvement, the mental health of parents is significantly improved, with less likelihood of child abuse or removal of children into statutory care.

Evaluation: Series of independent evaluation studies beginning in 1982. Continual assessment through NEWPIN centres, collection of routine statistics.

Publications: Various, since 1984. Most recent: Pound, A (1994) *NEWPIN: A Befriending and Therapeutic Network for Carers of Young Children.* HMSO.

Open University

Contact:

Mick Jones
School of Health and Social Welfare
The Open University
Walton Hall
Milton Keynes MK7 6AA   01908 654287

Description:

The OU has 17 years of experience of developing courses on parenting and childcare (for example, *The Pre-school Years, The First Years of Life, Parents and Teenagers*) and is currently developing a new *Parents and Under-8s* programme. This will consist of six modules, a group leaders' pack and a portfolio and assessment pack. The first modules will be available during 1996.

Funding:

So far, the Esmee Fairbairn Trust and the Baring Foundation.

Materials:

Each module built round a highly illustrated book which contains short, self-contained topics, allowing flexibility for group learning. Also audiotape and personal workbook.

Theoretical base:

Through a process of reflection and action, parents can be helped to build up their parenting skills.

Leader training:

The programme has associated group leader training and support. Participants will be encouraged to pass this on 'cascade fashion'.

Outcomes:

The OU estimates that 151,000 people were reached by the earlier *Pre-school Child* programme.

Evaluation:

Follow-up surveys showed that learners described knowledge gains; enhanced skills; changed attitudes; changed practice; increased self-confidence. Professionals and voluntary organisations found that the materials provided a flexible resource. Other social and community benefits were evident, through the empowerment of parents to take more active roles or to access further learning opportunities.

Publications:

Various. E.g. *A review of a collaborative health education programme 1976-1986*. A report for the Health Education Council. Open University.

Parent Effectiveness Training (PET)

Contact:	Val Winfield 147 Ware Road Hertford SG13 7EG 01992 582451
Description:	PET is a well-established programme, founded by psychologist Dr Thomas Gordon in California in 1965, and is widely used in Canada and the USA. There appear to be few courses currently running in the UK, although Gordon's ideas have been incorporated into other programmes. The objectives of the programme are to improve communication skills between parents and children, and increase the potential for loving relationships. The main topics in the eight-week course are: listening skills, talking, negotiating, anger and attention to anger, coping mechanisms, resolving conflicts.
Funding:	Participants pay around £75 per course.
Materials:	Textbook and workbook. Instructor manual.
Theoretical base:	Humanistic.
Leader training:	Intensive 60-hour programme covering the principles and teaching methods of PET. Instructors are not given full certification until successful teaching has been accomplished.
Outcomes:	For parents: huge weight of guilt removed, less stress and anger, more understanding and empathy, less teenage turmoil. For children: improved self-esteem, increased leadership qualities, better verbal skills, good negotiators, less whining.
Evaluation:	Various research reports.
Publications:	Gordon, T (1975) *Parent Effectiveness Training*. New York: Peter Wyden.

Parenthood Group

Contact:	Jane Mardon Deputy Education Co-ordinator Education Department Deerbolt Young Offenders Institution Bowles Road Barnard Castle Co Durham DL12 9BG 01833 37561 x 320
	Also John Wright and Debbie Twist at Lancaster Farms YOI who run a similar programme. Most prisons now run some sort of parenting course.
Description:	This programme started in 1985 and is for fathers and young men who are about to be fathers who are prisoners in the YOI (around 30 per cent of all inmates). Five 11-week courses are run per year (50 fathers) and a new four-week course has recently started. The course covers the practical side of childcare and also the emotional side of parenthood, relationships, taking on responsibilities, and so on. Many of the young men have literacy and numeracy problems, poor social skills and low self-image.
Funding:	Deerbolt YOI, Bishop Auckland College.
Materials:	Course material specially written.
Theoretical base:	Humanistic; social learning/behavioural; eclectic.
Leader training:	No specific training for this programme. Leaders are the Deputy Education Co-ordinator and the Head of the Basic Skills Department.
Outcomes:	Interviews indicated increase in knowledge of child development and positive changes in attitudes to family relationships.
Evaluation:	See above, as found in study by Caddle (1991).
Publications:	Caddle, D (1991) *Training for Fatherhood*. Home Office Research & Statistics Department Research Bulletin, 30, 35-39. Plus various articles, radio and TV programmes. Forthcoming: *Working with Men*, Longmans.

Parenting Course (Stockport)

Contact:	Lynda Dodd Educational Psychologist Educational Psychology Service Stockport Education Division Stopford House Town Hall Stockport SK1 3XE

0161 474 3870

Description: This course was first run in 1992 by Stockport's Educational Psychology Service. It is open to all parents and is based at nursery schools and primary schools, with 24-36 parents attending per year. Programmes average five two-hour sessions and crèches are provided. The aims of the course are to help people to cope better with the difficult job of parenting and to develop more positive relationships with their children. The sessions cover: childhood and parenthood; more effective communication; solving problems and developing self-discipline; play and learning; preparing for nursery or school; helping your child in school. On more recent courses the sessions have ended with parents and children coming together for a game/activity and a snack.

Funding: Stockport Educational Psychology Department

Materials: Specially written by EPs. Also use *Toddler Taming* by Christopher Green, and *Behaviour Can Change* by Westmacott and Cameron.

Theoretical base: Humanistic; social learning/behavioural; eclectic.

Leader training: Courses led by EPs, Portage worker and home-school liaison teacher, with one of the EPs being involved in all the courses so far.

Outcomes: Parents' self-reports by questionnaire, both straight after the course and a year later, indicate increased self-confidence and understanding of some of the skills of parenting. Particular reference was made to the value of listening to your child, focusing on the good points and enjoying being with your child.

Evaluation: Not yet written up.

Parent Network

Contact:

Carolyn Peters
Training & Development Manager
Parent Network
44-46 Caversham Road
London NW5 2DS   0171 485 8535

Description:

Parent Network was started in 1986. It provides education and support for parents through a programme called Parent-Link. The overall aim of Parent-Link is to develop self-aware and self-confident parents. Each parent who attends the Parent-Link programme is given a set of handbooks, one for each topic covered. Parents often continue in informal support groups and some attend follow-up modules such as sibling rivalry, anger management, living with teenagers and resolving conflicts. Over 200 Parent-Link Co-ordinators operate in around 30 local areas, and well over 10,000 people have attended a Parent-Link Programme.

Funding:

Charitable trusts and fees from trainee co-ordinators; participants' fees. Sometimes subsidies/funding from local authorities/health authorities etc.

Materials:

Handbooks to accompany the programme.

Theoretical base:

Humanistic, Rogerian, eclectic.

Leader training:

Facilitators are people who have already attended a Parent-Link group and have undertaken over 150 hours training over a six-month period. Further in-service training is available.

Outcomes:

Parents feel supported, have increased confidence and handle the stresses of family life more effectively. Children's self-esteem is raised and tension between parents and children can decrease.

Evaluation:

Parent-Link in the LB of Waltham Forest was evaluated by Mary Baginsky in 1993. Currently a one-year evaluation by Dr Hilton Davies at Guys Mental Health Unit. Due mid-1995.

Publications:

Sokolov, I and Hutton, D (1988) *The Parents Book* Thorsons (out of print).
Baginsky, M (1993) *Parent Link In Waltham Forest*. Baginsky Associates.

Parent Workshops (Southwark)

Contact: Tony Tarrant and Dilanthi Weerasinghe
                          London Borough of Southwark
                          Educational Psychology Service
                          Albany Annexe
                          Albany Road
                          London SE5 0BN   0171 525 2705

Description: This work started as a pilot project in two primary
                          schools in Southwark. The focus was originally on
                          processes, with the content consisting of play and
                          friendships, life skills, responsibilities and behaviour.

Funding: LEA Educational Psychology Service.

Materials: Handouts.

Theoretical base: Social learning/behavioural.

Parents Against Crime

Contact: Olivia Montuschi
Exploring Parenthood
4 Ivory Place
20A Treadgold Street
London W11 4PB   0171 221 4471

Description: This programme has been developed for use with parents whose children aged 10-14 are in trouble with the law or in school. Two courses have been run so far (in 1993), each attended by eight parents, all referred by social work agencies or Juvenile Justice Bureaux. Each course in the pilot project consisted of six two-hour sessions, although 12 sessions are recommended. A crèche and a youth group were provided alongside the parents' programme. The main objective of the PAC programme is to offer a series of theme-focused sessions which highlight the understanding and skills, (for example, communication, active listening, negotiation) which parents need in order to effect change.

Funding: Hammersmith & Fulham Safer Cities Project and Marks & Spencer funded the publication of a trainers' manual for the programme. Pilot PAC courses by the Home Office and various trusts.

Materials: *Parents Against Crime: Course Leader's Guide.* By Olivia Montuschi, Elizabeth Howell and Masana de Souza, Exploring Parenthood (1994).

Theoretical base: Social learning/behavioural; psychodynamic.

Leader training: EP offer one-day seminars and two-day training courses in using the leader's manual. The manual is not sold separately from the training.

Evaluation: Course leader's guide includes model parent referral forms and course evaluation forms.

Publications: Course Leader's Guide as details above.

The Parents and Children Series

Contact: Dr Stephen Scott
Children's Department
Maudsley Hospital
De Crespigny Park
Denmark Hill
London SE5 8AZ   0171 703 6333

Description: This approach is based on the work of Carolyn Webster-Stratton in Seattle. Through the use of video vignettes parents are helped to understand how their behaviour impacts upon their children. The objectives are to increase parental prasie for desired children's behaviour and teach non-punitive methods for undesired behaviour. There are normally 12 sessions each of two hours in a programme. The programme has been running in the UK since 1991.

Funding: Maudsley Hospital and Institute of Psychiatry. The Department of Health is currently funding a controlled trial of the method.

Materials: Series of video scenarios depicting parent–child situations developed in the USA. Have now been dubbed with English accents.

Theoretical base: Social learning/behavioural.

Leader training: The primary leader has to have completed two groups with a recognised trainer (Webster-Stratton's team).

Outcomes: For parents: increased feeling of control over children, reduced depression, high satisfaction, reduced incidence of smacking. For children: clinically and statistically significant reduction in both disruptive and emotional behaviour.

Evaluation: Just starting a controlled trial with 60 families in the group training programme and 60 receiving traditional therapy. Funded by the Department of Health.

Publications: None as yet from the Maudsley team, but in progress. Various from the Webster-Stratton team, most recently: Webster-Stratton, C (1994) *Advancing videotape parent training: a comparison study*. J Consult. Clin. Psychology 62, 3, 583-593.

Parents 'n' Kids

Contact:	Olivia Montuschi Training Courses Manager Exploring Parenthood 4 Ivory Place 20A Treadgold Street London W11 4PB 0171 221 4471
Description:	Parents 'n' Kids started in 1994 and is funded for three terms. It was developed as a direct result of the success of the Parents Against Crime Project. The programme for parents consists of 12 two-hour sessions. Children under eight are offered a parallel group with a high ratio of specialist staff. The objectives of the programme for both groups are to raise self-esteem in parents and children; to increase parenting skills; to improve family communication; to enable parents to devise a disciplinary framework to suit their family; to develop children's abilities to gain maximum benefit from their learning environment. The adult group focuses on issues identified by parents, building on their knowledge and understanding.
Funding:	Royal Borough of Kensington & Chelsea Social Services – one-off grant to cover costs of three 12-week courses.
Materials:	Mostly Exploring Parenthood's own material, but also makes use of *Positive Parenting* by E. Hartley-Brewer; *Parentmaking* by Rothenberg, A and others. California: Banster Press; and *Touchpoints* by T Berry Brazelton.
Theoretical base:	Humanistic; psychodynamic; social learning/behavioural.
Leader training:	Groupwork training at EP and Institute of Group Analysis; Counselling Diploma; Parent Counsellor.
Outcomes:	Too early to say.
Evaluation:	Parents complete short evaluation forms at the end of each session and a longer one at the end of the course.
Publications:	The whole project will be evaluated and written up. Guidelines for course leaders are being written.

Parentwise

Contact: Peter Jones
                          Community Psychologist
                          Co-ordinator, Parentwise Project
                          The Mannamead Centre
                          15 Eggbuckland Road
                          Plymouth PL3 5HF   01752 257981

Description: Parentwise is a community-based programme of education and support currently being developed in the Devonport are of Plymouth, a highly disadvantaged inner city area. The delivery of the programme is firmly based on a trans-agency approach, with a wide range of professional roles represented on the multi-agency group. Each of the sequential parent education modules is directed at parents of children within a given age band, and each is led by a key person from one agency with support from others. The current modules (*Enjoy your Baby, Walkers and Talkers, Stepping Out* and *Wise Words*) reflect a developmental model of parenting.

Funding: Principally from Plymouth & Torbay Health Authority. Support from West Devon Education Authority, Diocese of Exeter, West Devon Social Services and others.

Materials: Own material being developed. Parents' handouts and leaders' notes.

Theoretical base: Humanistic, eclectic, mediated learning experience.

Leader training: The professionals involved in the project share experiences of the whole process and are all committed to the mediation of the learning experience.

Outcomes: Programme still developing. Anecdotal evidence suggests that parents feel more confident of their parenting skills and gain greater rewards from being a parent.

Evaluation: The whole programme is the subject of a doctoral dissertation by Peter Jones. A parent survey is currently under way. This action research is examining how a programme of parent education and support might best reflect the needs of the given community as perceived by its members, the residents and the workers for statutory and voluntary agencies serving that community. Other members are involved in project-based research at MSc and other levels.

Publications: Articles: *Health Visitor* (1994) 6; CSLT Bulletin (1994) 12.

Parentwise (Birmingham)

Contact:	Judith Miller Parentwise Co-ordinator Birmingham Education Business Partnership c/o North Birmingham College Aldridge Road Great Barr Birmingham B44 8NE 0121 366 6733
Description:	Fifteen schools participated in this programme in 1993, with a further 15 involved in 1994/95. Each school developed around three courses, according to the needs and wishes of the parents. Few of these were specifically aimed at improving parenting skills *per se*. The programme was set up to offer parents the opportunity to develop personal skills, enabling them to actively support and participate in their children's education at all levels. There are plans to extend the programme to other areas of Birmingham.
Funding:	Birmingham Education Business Partnership and North Birmingham College.
Materials:	Varies according to programme.
Theoretical base:	Enhancing achievements by making parents more aware.
Leader training:	No specific training. Community tutors are generally trained to work with groups in a flexible way. Teachers and lecturers also involved in leading courses.
Outcomes:	Many parents claim to have gained in confidence and knowledge of the school environment. A number have progressed into full or part-time courses.
Evaluation:	Parents and schools self-reporting. Results have been written up. No external evaluation.
Publications:	Brochure.

PIPPIN (Parents in Partnership – Parent Infant Network)

Contact:	Mel Parr MA, C Couns Psychol 'Derwood' Todds Green Stevenage Herts SG1 2JE 01438 748478
Description:	PIPPIN (a registered charity) started in 1991 and is a structured, preventative, education and support programme which complements traditional antenatal classes. Its aim is to support the development of positive early family and parent-child relationships. PIPPIN groups begin around the fourth month of pregnancy, and there are four phases: Great Expectations, Review, Home Visit and Life after Birth. These comprise a total of 17 sessions, plus the home visit. Groups run on a freelance basis and within the NHS. The focus is on emotional support, communication and problem-solving skills, and sensitivity to the infant as a person.
Funding:	Artemis Trust. The cost is less than £100 per family.
Materials:	Specially designed parent notes only available to participants, to help build on ideas and skills in between sessions. Authors: Mel Parr and Barbara Morgan.
Theoretical base:	Humanistic, integrative, systemic.
Leader training:	Available to parents, para-professionals and professionals. Rigorous selection procedure, then over 200 hours over three terms. Moving towards an externally accredited award based on observed skills and competence in supporting parent-infant and couple relationships. Authorised facilitators receive manual and ongoing training, support and supervision.
Outcomes:	Better adjustment in terms of confidence as a parent; parent-infant relationship; separation anxiety; coping mechanisms, aspects of the parents' relationship. Two-three years later toddlers more calm and confident, and self-help support groups stilll running.
Evaluation:	PhD extensive Action Research Project – 50 couples in 9 intervention groups + 60 couples in control. M Parr (forthcoming). Process by which benefits are attained is evaluated. Ongoing monitoring/quality assurance in place; further long-term evaluation planned.

Publications: Parr, M. PhD forthcoming. Various articles, eg Parr, M (1995) 'PIPPIN' *Young Minds* Newsletter, 20, 15-16. Also presented at many conferences and in-service training seminars.

Positive Parenting

Contact: Sue Miller
                        Specialist Senior Educational Psychologist
                        Child Guidance Centre
                        Aykley Heads
                        Durham DH1 5TS   0191 386 5969

Description: This programme for parents is run as either single
                        workshops or a series, based on schools, community
                        centres, family centres etc. The six modules cover:
                        using existing strengths; obstacles to change; feeling
                        good about ourselves; planning for change; parents,
                        the flexible friends; working together. The objectives
                        are to empower parents to recognise their existing
                        skills and to prioritise and work systematically
                        towards clear, planned targets. A strong problem-
                        solving approach underpins all the materials, start-
                        ing with positives, working towards short and
                        long-term goals, and evaluation.

Funding: GEST; City Action/City Challenge. Employment Ser-
                        vices (Department of Employment)

Materials: *Positive Parenting*: handbook for parents. Six mod-
                        ules in ringbinder file, each including exercises and
                        assignments. Published by Formword Ltd, price £15

                        Positive Parenting: Training for Trainers. Durham
                        LEA.

Theoretical base: Social learning/behavioural; problem-solving approach.

Leader training: Training for Trainers course, and facilitators have a
                        proven track record of working effectively with young
                        children & their parents (for example, EP, teacher,
                        nursery nurse, health visitor, EWO, social worker,
                        parent).

Outcomes: Parents' self-reports indicated that they understood
                        their children better and felt more skilled as a parent.

Evaluation: Questionnaire feedback from parents before and after
                        the sessions. Evaluation by Felicity Penny, Univer-
                        sity of Northumbria SEN Resource Centre.

Publications: Article in *Bridges*, University of Northumbria, 1994.
                        RSA Parents in a Learning Society News No.4. Jour-
                        nal of Educational Psychology, January 1995.

Positive Parenting

Contact:	Carole Sutton, PhD Senior Lecturer in Psychology School of Health & Life Sciences De Montfort University Scraptoft Campus Leicester LE7 9SU 0116 255 1551
Description:	This programme has been developed for parents of difficult young children and formed the topic of Carole Sutton's PhD thesis in 1988. The study has been recently replicated, using a method of training parents by telephone. The objectives are to enable parents to manage their children in ways clearly validated by research leading to greater well-being for all concerned. The programme consists of a series of eight meetings with two follow-ups on specific skills of managing children.
Funding:	The author has funded most of the costs personally so far.
Materials:	*Managing Difficult Young Children* – a series of eight booklets. Published by Positive Parenting, P O Box 435, Leicester. Cost: £5, plus 50p post & packing.
Theoretical base:	Humanistic; Social learning/behavioural; Family systems.
Leader training:	Carole Sutton trains health visitors and social workers.
Outcomes:	For parents: reduction in levels of mothers' depression. For children: improvements in behaviour at post-intervention and follow-up at 12-18 months.
Evaluation:	Evaluation used independent assessors and statistical analysis. Four methods of parent training compared – group, home visit, telephone, wait list control. For all three intervention groups there was clinical improvement.
Publications:	Sutton, C (1992) 'Training parents to manage difficult children' *Behavioural Psychotherapy* 20, 115-139. Sutton, C (1995) 'Parent training by telephone: a partial replication!' *Behavioural and Cognitive Psychotherapy* 23, 1-24

Positive Parenting Packs

Contact:	Eileen Jones Portsmouth Area Family Concern 39 Wallington Road Portsmouth PO2 0HB 01705 382061
Description:	The Positive Parenting Packs 1 and 2 have been designed as resource material for group leaders. The idea for the packs came out of work with an Inner City Play Centre. The aim of the 20 articles is to provide a basis for discussion and then for parents to take them home one at a time. By December 1994 3,000 copies of the packs had been sold. The objectives of the packs are to give support and encouragement to parents; to give insight and to increase parenting skills; to provide resource material for group leaders.
Funding:	Sales of products, private donations, two small grants from local authority and two from IOF Child Abuse.
Materials:	*Positive Parenting Packs 1 and 2, New Beginnings Booklet, Did You Know? – You're special!, Robbed of Childhood, Positive Points for Parents* leaflets.
Theoretical base:	Social learning/behavioural; family systems; Judaeo/Christian value base.
Leader training:	Outline courses of five and ten weeks, based on *Positive Parenting Packs 1 & 2* being developed.
Outcomes:	For parents: recognition of the influence of their actions; insight into children's needs and motivations for change.
Evaluation:	Group leaders' and parents' response nationwide to questionnaire.
Publications:	Reviewed in various publications.

Promoting Positive Parenting

Contact: David Neville
Centre for Fun and Families
25 Shanklin Drive
Knighton
Leicester LE2 3RH   01533 707198

Description: The Centre for Fun and Families was set up in 1990 to assist families where parents are experiencing behaviour and communication difficulties with their children. It provides services direct to families and also by working alongside and training staff of statutory and voluntary agencies. The support is mainly through the formation of groupwork programmes. *Fun and Family Groups* and *Living with Teenagers* groups offer practical, down to earth advice aimed at enabling parents to reduce their children's poor behaviour and encourage more positive rewarding behaviour in its place. Parent groups using this approach are being run by 10 local authorities and several voluntary agencies.

Funding: Commercial activities of the Centre for Fun and Families.

Materials: Range of booklets, video and audiotapes, packs for group leaders.

Theoretical base: Social learning/behavioural.

Leader training: The Centre runs training and consultancy to train staff to run groups. Students on placement receive on-site training.

Outcomes: Average 50 per cent reduction in child behaviour difficulties during the seven weeks of the programme. Significant improvement in parental understanding and confidence.

Evaluation: A PhD student (Andy Gill) has researched the effectiveness of the groups. Being written up.

Publications: Gill, A (1989) 'Putting Fun back into Families' *Social Work Today*, 4 May, 14-15.

Neville, D, Beak, D and King, L (1995) *Promoting Positive Parenting*. Arena

Seven Supertactics for Superparents

Contact: Dr Frank Merrett
                      The University of Birmingham
                      School of Education
                      Edgbaston
                      Birmingham B15 2TT   0121 414 4866

Description: This booklet was originally devised by members of the
                      Association for Behavioural Approaches with Chil-
                      dren. Some 10,000 copies have been sold, but there is
                      no record of the way in which they have been used
                      with parents. At one time the authors used the con-
                      tents of the book on overhead transparencies and ran
                      a presentation for parents based on these. The book
                      describes strategies for parents to follow in bringing
                      up their children: rewards; copying others; guiding;
                      small steps; ignoring; removing child; removing
                      rewards.

Funding: Sales of booklet.

Materials: Wheldall, K, Wheldall, D and Winter, S (1986) *Seven
                      Supertactics for Superparents*. Positive Products.

Theoretical base: Social learning/behavioural.

Publications: As above.

Special Parenting Programme

Contact:	Dr Sue McGaw Head of Special Parenting Service 57 Pydar Street Truro Cornwall TR1 2SS 01872 72494
Description:	The Special Parenting Service (SPS) was started in 1988 by Sue McGaw and works with parents who have learning disabilities. In addition to specialist home teaching, parents are invited to attend a weekly group for 16 weeks. About 40 parents attend per year. Topics cover parents' self-esteem, relationships, contraception, childcare, behaviour management, symptom recognition, emergency responses, feeding and sexual abuse. Peer support and community integration are actively encouraged.
Funding:	Health Authority. Operated by the Cornwall and Isles of Scilly Learning Disabilities NHS Trust.
Materials:	Based on the LIFE programme, by L Anderson, Developmental Services Centre, Champaign, USA.
Theoretical base:	Social learning/behavioural; family systems.
Leader training:	Course delivered by clinical psychologists, trained by Dr McGaw and through standard courses such as Portage Course.
Outcomes:	For parents: improved knowledge of childcare. Improved self-esteem. For children: better personal care.
Evaluation:	No external evaluation but the team are in the process of writing up their work.
Publications:	McGaw, S and Sturmey, P (1993) *Identifying the Needs of Parents with Learning Disabilities: A Review* Child Abuse Review, 2, 101-117. McGaw, S and Sturmey, P (1994) *Assessing Parents with Learning Disabilities: The Parental Skills Model* Child Abuse Review, 3, 1-16. Video: *Learning to be Mum*. Arrowhead Productions.

Systematic Training for Effective Parenting (STEP)

Contact:
Norma Angeli
Health Visitor
Health Centre
Rodney Road
Walton-on-Thames
Surrey KT12 3LB   01932 228999

Description:
This programme is offered by health visitors to all parents with children under five in Walton-on-Thames. The aim of the scheme is to make it normal to attend a course in parenting, and to positively improve the effectiveness of the parent-child relationship. This health visitor started running these programmes in 1989, and four health visitors now run six courses per year, with over 50 parents attending per year. The programme uses the well-established American STEP programme developed by Dinkmeyer and McKay in the 1970s. The STEP programme consists of nine topics. The health visitors in Surrey generally run six sessions as a course.

Funding:
Weybourne NHS Trust.

Materials:
Parents' Handbook, Parenting Younger Children, Parenting Teens. All by Dinkmeyer, D and McKay, G. American Guidance Service. Circle Pines, Minnesota, USA.

Theoretical base:
Psychoanalytic; family systems.

Leader training:
Specific training programme in facilitation of groups and in the use of STEP published by the American Guidance Service, and developed by Weybourne NHS Trust for training health visitors.

Outcomes:
Parents are happier with their children. They describe one behaviour that has changed for the better.

Evaluation:
Parent self-reports by postal questionnaire for 1991 and 1992, 3-6 months after the end of the course.

Publications:
Angeli, N and others (1994) 'Facilitating parenting skills in vulnerable families' *Health Visitor* 67, 4, 130-132.

Allan, J (1994) 'Parenting Education' *Children & Society,* 8,4 344-359.

Toddler Taming and Behaviour Management

Contact: Early Learning Support Team
c/o Priory Campus
Pontefract Road
Lundwood
Barnsley S71 5PN   01226 770621

Description: This programme is operated by the Early Learning Support Team in Barnsley, and was first run in 1994. It is held in a local nursery school and is open to all parents. About 36 parents attended the four programmes in 1994. The objectives are to develop confidence in parents and carers in dealing with their children's behaviour. The programme covers general behaviour management techniques, the ABC of behaviour and specific behaviour problems.

Funding: Barnsley City Challenge and the LEA.

Materials: *Toddler Taming*, by Dr Christopher Green (1993). Vermilion.

Theoretical base: Social learning/behavioural; family systems.

Leader training: The course is led by a team of qualified and experienced Nursery Nurses who have trained in Portage work and Adult Further Education Teacher's Certificate.

Outcomes: For parents: more confidence, less stress, improved relationships with children. For children: more cooperative, happier and increased self-esteem.

Evaluation: None so far.

Publications: None.

Working with Parents for Change

Contact: Penny Edwards and Lynn Townsend
                    Educational Psychologists
                    Renfrew Psychological Service
                    Carbrook Street
                    Paisley PA1 2NW   0141 887 7821

Description: This package was originally designed in 1987 by two
                    educational psychologists for parents of young chil-
                    dren with behavioural difficulties. It became clear
                    that it was helpful to all parents, and that it could be
                    used for parents of older children too. The programme
                    is run in Pre-5 Units in Strathclyde. Courses are gen-
                    erally of eight-twelve units each of two hours dura-
                    tion. The objectives are to help parents understand
                    the emotional and social needs of children, to become
                    aware of parents' needs (and possible conflict here),
                    and to give advice on how to handle behavioural diffi-
                    culties.

Funding: Strathclyde Regional Council Psychological Service.

Materials: Package *Working with Parents for Change* by
                    Edwards, P & Townsend, L (1993) Strathclyde
                    Regional Council. Contains Leader's Handbook and
                    four topic booklets: *Parenting, Handling Difficult
                    Behaviour, Families, Developmental Issues.*

Theoretical base: Social learning/behavioural; family systems; eclectic.

Leader training: Usually group leaders attend a series of nine weekly
                      half-day meetings led by the original authors, and
                      plans to 'cascade' this learning.

Outcomes: For parents: greater self-esteem and control, leading
                    to better relationships in family. For children: some
                    improvement in behaviour as a result of more sensi-
                    tive, quieter handling.

Evaluation: Internal monitoring system in place. Also small eval-
                    uation by a student at Strathclyde University.

Publications: Edwards, P and Townsend, L (1987) 'Pre-school
                    behaviour problems: a model of intervention'. *Psycho-
                    logical Initiatives.*

Appendix II

Summaries of evaluations of parenting skills programmes

ABC: A study of behaviour management workshops for parents of nursery school children

Author: Hinton (1988)

Aims: To analyse the methodology and content of the workshops and to produce a curriculum and course material to facilitate replication;
To evaluate changes following workshop intervention:
a)   in child behaviour at home
b)   in child behaviour at school
c)   in mother's self-esteem
d)   in mothers' knowledge of behavioural strategies

Sample: Five workshop courses in LEA schools (six x one-hour sessions). 32 mother/child pairs selected for study, divided into workshop and control groups.

Methodology: Three questionnaires aimed to determine the degree of the child's behaviour disorder (Richman and Graham's Behavioural Screening Questionnaire); mother's knowledge of behavioural strategies (Behavioural Strategies Test); mother's level of self-esteem and feeling of competence in her parenting role (Battle's Culture-Free Self Esteem Inventory Form AD). Child's behaviour in school also assessed by class teacher (McGuire & Richman Pre-school Behaviour Checklist). Before and after data collected.

Findings: Cautious optimism that:
1)   the number of behaviour difficulties as reported by the mother decreases.
2)   the number of behaviour difficulties reported by teachers decreases.
3)   parents' knowledge of behavioural strategies increases.

Coping with Kids

Publication: Coping with Kids Annual Report 1993-94. Describes Assertive Discipline (AD) courses for parents in some of the most deprived areas of Bristol.

Aims: Whether AD was effective in giving parents new strategies for managing their children;
Whether it was viable to run such courses in a systematic way;
Whether AD was attractive to parents living under stress.

Sample: Five courses each run for three sessions (80 families)

Methodology: Self-completion questionnaires at end of third session.

Findings: Almost all parents felt they had benefited (many reported being calmer), and many reported immediate changes in their children's behaviour.

Coping with Kids (Kidderminster)

Authors: Bradley and Weller (1994)

Aims: To examine effect of the six sessions on parents' confidence and enjoyment of seven aspects of parenting. (Having fun; Success in obtaining obedience; Taking child to meet family and friends; Confidence in parenting well; Enjoying child's company; Ideas for play activities; Progress in changing child's behaviour.)

Sample: Six families attending the course.

Methodology: Self-completion questionnaires by parents.

Findings: Three of the six families reported big changes in the 'confidence and enjoyment' indices. Two reported small improvements; one reported a negative change.

Effective Parenting Programme for Schools (Hartley-Brewer and Hills)

Author: Pugh (1994).

Aims: The effectiveness of the training course in transferring general competence and groupwork skills;

The appropriateness and accessibility of the materials, for both parents and facilitators;

The programme's impact on parents and children; on schools as perceived by the head teacher, facilitator, other staff and the LEA; and on improved home-school links;

Some analysis of parent participation rates, related in particular to the social and ethnic composition of school populations.

Sample: Sixteen schools running five topic courses.

Methodology: Self-reporting from parents after attending course; Questionnaires for head teachers, facilitators and LEA advisers.

Findings:	a) Training course effective in transferring general competence and groupwork skills to facilitators;
	b) Appropriateness and accessibility of materials very highly rated by facilitators and by majority of parents who completed evaluation forms;
	c) 76 per cent of parents who completed questionnaires (half the total) found sessions 'very useful'.

Everyday Problems in Childhood

Author: Clench (1994).

Sample: A group of parents with children with special educational needs, meeting for six sessions.

Methodology: Interview with group organiser immediately after formal meetings had finished; maintained contact with one group member; interviewed five parents one year after formal meetings finished.

Findings: Affective: acceptance of problem; no longer alone; new confidence; improved self-image; assertive.

Practical: three specific problems 'solved'; mutual support; continued regular meetings; further EPIC group; other initiatives.

Overall, parents felt empowered.

Handling Children's Behaviour

Author: Lawes (1992).

Aims: To evaluate an individual parent training programme implemented by nursery staff.

Sample: Eight mothers and their pre-school children; matched group of 9 mothers; control group of 11 given reading material on child development and took part in discussion group.

Methodology: Pre- and post-test measures on self-esteem (SES), parental attitude towards children (PAS), knowledge of behavioural principles (KBP), pre-school behaviour checklist on children (PSBC).

Findings: Significant improvement pre- to post-test in 1) PAS and KBP for individual training; 2) PAS, SES and PSBC for group training. No change in control group

Mellow Mothering: Intervention based on the NEWPIN model

Authors: Puckering and others (1994).

Aims: To study effects of the intervention on mothers and children.

Sample: Twenty one mothers (a further seven dropped out). Six families, involving 12 children, were on the at-risk register.

Methodology: Observational data from pre- and post-group videotapes (using following dimensions – anticipation, mother's positive affect, mother's negative affect, mother link-child follow, autonomy);

Anonymous feedback of self-report measures;

Registration and deregistration from the Child Protection Register.

Findings: Last four observational measures showed changes in the expected direction. Positive changes in children's and own behaviour reported. 10 of the 12 children had been removed from the CPR.

Parent-Link in Waltham Forest

Author: Baginsky (1993).

Aims: To identify the benefits or otherwise of Parent-Link to participants and to identify the factors which contributed to the effectiveness while determining which aspects, if any, could be improved.

Sample: Eight courses in the Borough between February and July 1993 (65 parents).

Methodology: Parents completed questionnaires at the introductory session, after the first or second session and after the final session. In addition, 20 face-to-face interviews and 15 telephone interviews with parents were carried out. Five of the latter were with parents who had not completed the course.

Findings: The overwhelming majority of parents found the courses useful and enjoyable. The help they had received included the following:

- 81% said the course had helped them reach a better understanding of their children's feelings;
- 75% said the course had helped them to communicate with their children;
- 72% said the course had helped them to a better understanding of their children's behaviour;
- 42% said they were in a better position to deal with behaviour problems in children.

Parents and Children Series

Authors: Routh and others (in preparation).

Aims: To understand the predictors of outcomes for parent management training, i.e relationship between attachment status and treatment outcome.

Sample: 37 mothers of children aged 5-9 with conduct disorder.

Methodology: Adult Attachment Interview Schedule 13-43 months after treatment. Standardised ratings, using Eyberg Child Behaviour Inventory) were made of behaviour problems prior to treatment, after attending the group and at follow-up. Maternal psychopathology (General Health Questionnaire) and marital adjustment (Dyadic Adjustment Scale) were also assessed at follow-up.

Findings: Behavioural outcome best predicted by a regression model that included the level of problem at referral, psychosocial stress index, and resolved versus unresolved maternal attachment ratings. That is for the group with unresolved attachment, the greater the problem at referral the greater the improvement in behaviour after parent training.

PIPPIN

Author: Parr (forthcoming).

Aims: To test effect of the PIPPIN intervention on adjustment to the transition to parenthood.

Sample: 47 expectant couples for Phase 1; 60 couples for Phase 2.

Methodology: Large number of measures: Social & Family History Questionnaire; Childhood and Family History; Parent Bonding Instrument; Reproductive Health and History; Parental Role Model; Parental Role Investment; Parental Separation Anxiety; Beliefs about control of pain; Career salience. Outcome measures: Obstetric Complication Score; General Health and Stresses; Physical & Emotional Wellbeing; Social Support Network scale; Issues and Concerns; Interpersonal Sensitivity Measure; Postnatal Depression Scale; Pregnancy Research Questionnaire and others.

Findings: Better adjustment in terms of: confidence as a parent, parent-infant relationship, separation anxiety, coping mechanisms, aspects of the couple relationship.

Positive Parenting

(i)

Author: Penny (1994).

Aims: To consider the effectiveness of the training in terms of changing parents' views;
Ascertain the views of head teachers;
Consider the feasibility of the long-term effectiveness of the project.

Sample: 18 parents (two had not attended) and six head teachers.

Methodology: Interviews and self-completion evaluation sheets.

Findings: Parents recognised that they were already experienced in the highly complex skills of parenting;
Parents learned new approaches to child management;
Parents felt valued partners in their children's development;
Parents felt valued adults who were worthy of investment and training.

(ii)

Author:	Dawson (1995).

Aims: To consider the effectiveness of the course by examining how successful it is in meeting its own aims;

To discover the reasons parents come on the course;

To discover parents' expectations of the course and whether they felt these had been met.

To look at the possibility of the course effecting long term change in parenting.

Sample: 10 parents attending, or who had attended, Positive Parenting groups at four schools.

Methodology: Structured interview with each parent and with head teachers.

Findings: Parents came on the course because they were having difficulties dealing with their children's behaviour;

The course made parents think about and change their own behaviour.

Parents were happy with the course content, and the course materials gave a focus to the group;

Parents and teachers reported that there had been observable and long-lasting change in the behaviour of children (and parents) due to the course.

Training parents to manage difficult children: a comparison of methods

Author: Sutton (1992)

Aims: Behavioural training of parents (ABC) by three methods: group, home visit and telephone (+ control).

Sample: 41 families pre-intervention, 39 post-intervention, 20 at follow-up 12-18 months later.

Methodology: Child Behaviour Questionnaire

Home situations questionnaire

Personal stress score sheet

Tarler-Benlolo test of understanding of principles of social learning theory.

Negative count of child failing to comply with instruction.

Positive Count of child complying with instruction.

Goal compliance – movement towards goal.

Findings: Possible to train parents of difficult pre-school children to manage them effectively by means of eight two-hour sessions.

Children more manageable compared with children of parents who did not receive training.

Effects of training persisted at 12-18 months as reported by independent evaluators.

Falling away (most in the telephone method) in the maintenance of effects.

Little to choose between methods of training.

Working with Parents for Change

Author: Redpath (1991)

Aims: To address four main research questions:

Is there a need for intervention of some kind at this stage?

Is this an effective method of intervention?

Can change be observed in the child's behaviour, or in the parent's perception of the behaviour?

Does there appear to be any change in the parents themselves either in the way they handle the child, or more generally?

How do parents feel about the group before and after?

Have the mothers' perceptions of parenting changed?

Sample: Three parent groups, providing a sample of 11 mothers in total.

Methodology: Pre- and post-intervention interviews with parents.

Findings: The intervention programme appeared to have helped mothers develop knowledge and understanding of the factors affecting children's behaviour; examine and enhance their parenting skills; learn alternative strategies for managing children's behaviour. The programme also appeared to have a positive effect on the psychological well-being of the mothers.

Appendix III

Useful organisations

This Appendix includes only those organisations which have a direct involvement in parenting education. Other organisations can be found in Appendix I in association with specific parenting programmes.

All-Party Parliamentary Group on Parenting
c/o Exploring Parenthood
4 Ivory Place
20A Treadgold Street
London
W11 4PB

Barnardo's
Tanners Lane
Barkingside
Essex IG6 1QC

Carlton Television
101 St Martin's Lane
London
WC2N 4AZ
(Videotape available: *Getting Through the Day*)

Crime Concern
Signal Point
Station Road
Swindon
Wiltshire SN1 1FE

Exploring Parenthood
4 Ivory Place
20A Treadgold Street
London W11 4PB

Family Service Units
207 Old Marylebone Road
London NW1 5QP

Health Visitors Association
50 Southwark Street
London SE1 1UN

Home-Start UK
2 Salisbury Road
Leicester LE1 7QR

Methodist Church Division of Education and Youth
2 Chester House
Pages Lane
Muswell Hill
London N10 1PR

National Childbirth Trust
Alexandra House
Oldham Terrace
Acton
London W3

Parenting Education and Support Forum
National Children's Bureau
8 Wakley Street
London EC1V 7QE

Parentline
Rayia House
57 Hart Road
Thundersly
Essex SS7 3PD

Parents & Co
25 Leighton Road
London NW5 2QD

Pre-school Learning Alliance
61-63 Kings Cross Road
London WC1X 9LL

Promoting Parenting Skills
David Scott
Psychology Department
Chester College of Higher Education
Cheyney Road
Chester CH1 4BJ

Relate
Herbert Gray College
Little Church Street
Rugby
Warwickshire CV21 3AP

Rapport
1A Forum Buildings
St James Parade
Bath BA1 1UG

Stepfamily
National Stepfamily Association
1 Chapel House
18 Hatton Place
London EC1N 8RU

Index

Entries are arranged in letter-by-letter order (hyphens and spaces between words are ignored).